The Growth Strategies of Hotel Chains
of Hotel Chains
Best Business Practices
by Leading Companies

The Growth Strategies of Hotel Chains
Best Business Practices by Leading Companies

Onofre Martorell Cunill, PhD

THHP

The Haworth Hospitality Press®
An Imprint of The Haworth Press, Inc.
New York • London • Oxford

For more information on this book or to order, visit
http://www.haworthpress.com/store/product.asp?sku=5387

or call 1-800-HAWORTH (800-429-6784) in the United States and Canada
or (607) 722-5857 outside the United States and Canada

or contact orders@HaworthPress.com

Published by

The Haworth Hospitality Press®, an imprint of The Haworth Press, Inc., 10 Alice Street, Binghamton, NY 13904-1580.

PUBLISHER'S NOTE
The development, preparation, and publication of this work has been undertaken with great care. However, the Publisher, employees, editors, and agents of The Haworth Press are not responsible for any errors contained herein or for consequences that may ensue from use of materials or information contained in this work. The Haworth Press is committed to the dissemination of ideas and information according to the highest standards of intellectual freedom and the free exchange of ideas. Statements made and opinions expressed in this publication do not necessarily reflect the views of the Publisher, Directors, management, or staff of The Haworth Press, Inc., or an endorsement by them.

Cover design by Jennifer M. Gaska.

Library of Congress Cataloging-in-Publication Data

Martorell Cunill, Onofre.
   The growth strategies of hotel chains : best business practices by leading companies / Onofre Martorell Cunill.
      p. cm.
   Includes bibliographical references and index.
   ISBN-13: 978-0-7890-2663-7 (hc. : alk. paper)
   ISBN-10: 0-7890-2663-5 (hc. : alk. paper)
   ISBN-13: 978-0-7890-2664-4 (pbk. : alk. paper)
   ISBN-10: 0-7890-2664-3 (pbk. : alk. paper)
      1. Hotel management. I. Title.

TX911.3.M3C86 2005
647.94'068—dc22
                                                                        2005002281

To my parents, Miquel and Cati,
to my brother Rafel, and to Nuria

Well, brothers and sisters, ladies and gentlemen, you don't need me to tell you that honors are won at the expense of great fatigue.

CONTENTS

Acknowledgments   ix

Chapter 1. The Concept of a Strategy   1

Chapter 2. Competitive Strategies   5

Chapter 3. Diversification versus Specialization   17

Chapter 4. Vertical Integration   37

Chapter 5. Horizontal Integration   51

Chapter 6. Diagonal Integration   69

Chapter 7. Acquisitions and Mergers   73

Chapter 8. Strategic Alliances: The Case of Joint Ventures   95

Chapter 9. Franchise Contracts   111

Chapter 10. Management Contracts   127

Chapter 11. Leaseholds and Ownership   145

Chapter 12. Branding   149

Chapter 13. The Internationalization-Globalization
of Hotel Chains   169

Notes   191

Bibliography   201

Index   207

ABOUT THE AUTHOR

Onofre Martorell Cunill, PhD, also holds master's degrees in business administration and economic-financial management. He is a lecturer at the University of the Balearic Islands in the Faculty of Business and Management Administration, the School of Business Studies, the Official Tourism School, the Higher Studies in Tourism program, and the MBA and MTA programs. He is also a lecturer at the Financial Institute of Madrid, the International Center of Financial Studies, the Business School ESADE (Barcelona), and the University of Alicante, all in Spain. He has served as an advisor to several international hotel chains and is the author of *Hotel Chains: Analysis of the TOP 10,* as well as of a large number of articles for national and international workshops.

Acknowledgments

I am indebted to a multitude of different people and institutions, since any work is the result of numerous prior contributions and influences: the teachers I have had, whom I am always pleased to remember, reading matter on the subject that was studied and pondered over again and again, and, of course, the University of the Balearic Islands, to which I give my most heartfelt thanks.

Some personal contributions must be given express mention: Dr. Antoni Aguiló, to whom I am very grateful for guiding my work with his advice the entire time, and Dr. Eugeni Aguiló, whose clear-sightedness and enthusiasm played a major role in the work's completion.

I would also like to thank Sol Meliá executives, Mr. Onofre Servera, Mr. Rafael Pascual, and Mr. Gaspar Llabrés, for their valuable assistance.

Finally I wish to thank my parents for yet again finding the strength to assist me. I am very proud to dedicate this work to them and to my brother Rafel.

Also, many thanks to all those who made this work possible by forgiving my long absences.

Chapter 1

The Concept of a Strategy

What is a strategy? No definition is universally accepted. The term is used by many authors with different meanings. For example, some include targets and goals as part of the strategy, while others establish clear distinctions between them.

James Brian Quinn (Mintzberg and Quinn, 1993) gives special emphasis to the military uses of the word, and he highlights a series of "dimensions" or criteria from this field that are crucial if strategies are to be successful. To illustrate these criteria, the writer refers to the times of Philip II and Alexander of Macedonia, the origin of his main example. Quinn also presents a summarized theory of how similar concepts to those used then influenced subsequent military and diplomatic strategies.

No one can deny that the military aspects of strategy have always been a subject of discussion and part of our universal literature. In fact the origin of the word "strategy" goes back to the Greeks who were conquered by Alexander the Great and his father.

Initially the word *strategos* was used to refer to a specific rank (the commander in chief of an army). Later it came to mean "the general's skills," or the psychological aptitude and character skills with which he carried out the appointed role. In the time of Pericles (450 BC), it referred to administrative skills (management, leadership, oratory, and power), and in the days of Alexander the Great (330 BC) the term was used to refer to the ability to apply force, overcome the enemy, and create a global, unified system of government.

Mintzberg concentrates on several different definitions of strategy, as a *plan* (i.e., a maneuver), *pattern, position,* and *perspective* (Mintzberg and Quinn, 1993). The author uses the first two definitions to

1

take readers beyond the concept of a *deliberate* strategy, moving far away from the traditional meaning of the word to the notion of an emerging strategy. With it, Mintzberg introduces the idea that strategies can be *developed* within an organization without anyone consciously proposing to do so or making a proposal as such. In other words, they are not *formulated*. Although this seems to contradict what is already established in published literature on strategy, Mintzberg maintains that many people implicitly use the word this way, even though they would not actually define it so.

In the world of management, a "strategy" is a pattern or plan that encapsulates the main goals and policies of an organization, while also establishing a coherent sequence of actions to be put into practice. A well-formulated strategy facilitates the systemization and allocation of an organization's resources, taking into account the organization's internal strong points and its shortcomings so as to achieve a viable, unique situation and also to anticipate potential contextual changes and unforeseen action by intelligent rivals.

Even though each strategic situation is different, do some common criteria tend to define what makes a good strategy? Simply because a strategy has worked, it cannot be used to judge another. Was it the Russians' strategy in 1968 that enabled them to crush the Czechs? Of course other factors (including luck, abundant resources, highly intelligent or plainly stupid orders or maneuvers, and mistakes by the enemy) contribute toward certain end results.

Some studies propose certain basic criteria for assessing a strategy (Tilles, 1963; Christenson, Andrews, and Bower, 1978). These include a clear approach, motivating effects, internal coherence, contextual compatibility, the availability of the necessary resources, the degree of risk, coherence with key managers' personal values, a suitable time frame, and applicability. Furthermore, by looking at historic examples of strategy from military, diplomatic, and business scenarios, we can infer that effective strategies must also include a minimum number of other basic factors and elements, such as

- clear, decisive objectives;
- the ability to retain the initiative;
- concentration;
- flexibility;

- a coordinated, committed sense of leadership;
- surprise; and
- security.

These fundamental aspects of strategy apply, whether we are talking about business, government organization, or military campaigns.

Chapter 2

Competitive Strategies

THE THEORY

Porter suggests that generic competitive strategies are based on what he calls the factors that determine competition or, in other words, based on an analysis of the competitive environment. He comments that the competitive situation of a specific industrial sector depends on five fundamental competitive forces (Porter, 1982):

1. The threat of new entry by potential competitors
2. The threat of substitute products or services
3. Clients' bargaining power
4. Suppliers' bargaining power
5. Rivalry among the current competitors

Figure 2.1 shows the different forces that affect competition in an industrial sector.

These five competitive forces together determine the intensity of competition and the profitability of the industrial sector. The strongest force (or forces) is the one that heads the field, and it plays a crucial role in the development of a strategy.[1]

Porter (1982) describes a competitive strategy as taking offensive or defensive action to create a secure position in an industrial sector, so as to deal successfully with the five competitive forces, thereby obtaining greater company returns on the capital invested.

Business managers have discovered many different ways of achieving this goal and, on an individual level, the best strategy is a unique formula that reflects the company's specific circumstances. However, on a wider level, three internally consistent generic strategies can be identified and analyzed. These can be used singly or in combination

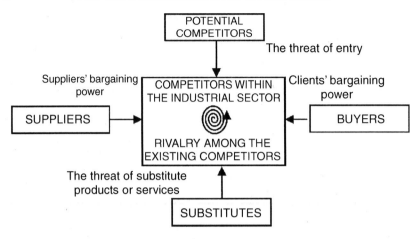

FIGURE 2.1. The Forces That Affect Competition in an Industrial Sector

to create a long-term secure position and distinguish the firm from rivals operating in the same sector.

Several methods can ensure that an effective strategy achieves this secure position, thus protecting the company against the five competitive forces. They include (1) positioning the company so that its capabilities offer the best defense against the existing competitive forces; (2) influencing the balance of these forces via strategic movements, thus improving the business's relative position; and (3) anticipating and responding swiftly to changes in the factors on which these forces depend, then choosing a strategy more consistent with the new competitive balance before rivals see this possibility.

An important aspect of an analysis of Porter's competitive strategies (1982) is the *value chain.* With it, company leaders should be able to identify what activities they can influence in order to bring about one of the proposed competitive strategies. From a definition of what a competitive strategy is, an analysis of the five competitive forces or factors that determine competition, and the idea of a value chain, three generic competitive strategies can be described: *cost leadership strategy, differentiation strategy,* and *focus or market niche strategy.*

The first two strategies are suitable for rival companies competing in an entire sector or industry, whereas the third is appropriate for companies competing in a particular segment of an industrial sector or market.

Figure 2.2 shows these generic competitive strategies.

Cost Leadership

With a cost leadership strategy, the idea is to gain a competitive edge by achieving a cost advantage. In other words, you must reduce your costs as much as possible. This gives the company an advantage over its rivals and also over its suppliers and clients. To develop this strategy, several conditions are required:

- The company must have a high market share so that it has a high volume of sales. In this way the managers can benefit from learning and experience.
- The leaders must ensure the high performance of those factors that permit a reduction in the unit cost of production.
- Technology must be used to ensure that goods are made at the lowest possible cost.
- If possible, the company managers must try to carry out a policy of product standardization to achieve high production levels and, therefore, a lower unit cost.

Entry barriers are one way of contributing toward the strategy's success, in the form of economies of scale and a cost advantage in production and distribution. This strategy allows a company to achieve a stronger position than its rivals, because the company's low costs allow executives to cut prices while continuing to make a profit until their closest rival's profit margins disappear. The company's wider

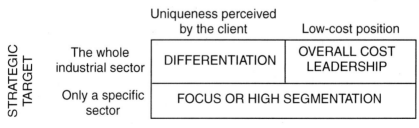

STRATEGIC ADVANTAGE

		Uniqueness perceived by the client	Low-cost position
STRATEGIC TARGET	The whole industrial sector	DIFFERENTIATION	OVERALL COST LEADERSHIP
	Only a specific sector	FOCUS OR HIGH SEGMENTATION	

FIGURE 2.2. The Three Generic Strategies

margins and greater size allow for bargaining with suppliers so that, even if the latter were to force a price increase, the company would still have a cost advantage.

Nevertheless, this strategy has risks. If it is followed consistently but measures are not taken to guarantee the continuance of the previous conditions, serious dangers could arise. As changes in technology occur, the firm's technology and production levels must be adapted to respond to new requirements. Should this not happen, the company could lose its cost advantage if a rival incorporates these changes instead.

Neither should the company leaders disregard their products' possible obsolescence or clients' new expectations. In addition, the strategy's[2] drawbacks also include the limited validity of the experience curve when a big change occurs in technology or when new entrants are able to learn more swiftly.

If company owners wish to achieve a cost advantage by reducing their total costs, an activity analysis can be very effective. It highlights activity-generated costs, activity components, and links between activities and chains of suppliers or clients that can be modified in order to contribute toward a decrease in costs.

The Differentiation Strategy

The aim of the differentiation strategy is to ensure that either the company in general or certain specific elements (such as its products, customer care, quality, etc.) are perceived to be unique by both clients and suppliers. As one might suppose, this kind of strategy means that the company involved must have certain capacities and skills (i.e., technology, marketing, etc.) that enable it to achieve, maintain, and develop a certain degree of differentiation.[3]

As for the clients, this strategy attempts to instill a sense of client loyalty toward the company and its products and services, making the demand less sensitive to price fluctuations. Differentiation permits higher prices and wider margins than companies without it could allow themselves. In turn, these wider margins help to ensure better bargaining power over suppliers and clients. Although exceptions exist, using this type of strategy normally makes it difficult to achieve a high market share.

The value chain is equally useful in the differentiation strategy. In this case, an analysis must be made of the activities involved in the value chain and their links in order to determine which of their basic characteristics can be modified so as to differentiate the company from its competitors.

The Focus or Market Niche Strategy

The focus or market niche strategy is based on the concept of concentrating on a certain segment of the market, thus limiting the scope of competition. Once a company is positioned in a market niche, the executives must try to achieve a position of leadership by cutting costs, by differentiation, or by both means, thereby trying to obtain a competitive advantage within the market segment or niche in which they are competing.

Companies that achieve a high degree of segmentation will also be able to obtain higher average profits in their particular sector.[4] The market niche strategy has the following risks: (1) An increase in the cost differential between competitors focusing on the whole market and companies following a market niche strategy eliminates the cost advantages of focusing on a limited target segment, or offsets the differentiation that was achieved by concentrating on one particular segment. (2) Differences can be found in the products or services really required by the target segment. (3) Rivals find submarkets within the target segment and outfocus the focuser.

Relevant Factors in Employing the Strategies

Other differences characterize the three generic strategies as well as those aspects already discussed. For the strategies' successful application a number of different resources and skills are required, involving different types of organization, control procedures, and incentive systems.

A global analysis of Porter's competitive strategies reveals a certain association with company size, meaning that cost leadership and differentiation strategies are more suitable for big companies or those with easy access to the resources needed to apply them. On the other hand, small or medium-sized companies seem more suited to market niche or focus strategies. However, this strategy could also be used by big companies, although not exclusively as our analysis showed.

Company leaders might decide to use the differentiation strategy in combination with the market niche strategy. Indeed in many cases to do so is even advantageous (Wright, 1987).

Nevertheless, as Porter comments, a hybrid strategy incorporating some aspects of a cost leadership strategy and others based on differentiation must be avoided. He calls this a "mid position." Although this situation does not imply the strategy's total failure, it does mean less effective performance than if one of the two strategies had been chosen instead (Porter, 1982).[5]

More recently, Wright (1987) qualified the belief that the differentiation strategy signifies a reduced market share and very high profit levels by stating that leaders of big companies with a high market share develop differentiation strategies and manage to achieve high profit levels. The following section will examine how these competitive strategies have been applied by the international hotel trade's leading hotel chains.

EXAMPLES

Cost Leadership Strategy

The following are examples of leading international hotel chains that have chosen to introduce the cost leadership competitive strategy for some of their brand names.

Cendant Corporation

Cendant Corporation has, among others, the following five brand names.

Super 8 Motels. This chain was founded in 1974. It was given this name because the first hotel to open under this brand name charged an average daily room (ADR) of $8.88. Super 8 Motels owns a total of 125,844 hotel rooms in 2,076 U.S. motels, making it the company brand name with the most hotels.

Travelodge Hotels. This brand name was created in 1935. It has 598 hotels with approximately 47,688 reasonably priced rooms throughout the United States.[6] This type of hotel is directed at both business travelers and tourists.

Knights Inn. Founded in 1972, this hotel chain has nearly 205 hotels and a total of 15,540 rooms. It offers limited hotel services and is focused on clients with a medium level of purchasing power who travel during the course of their work. Its marketing strategy focuses on long-distance truck drivers. For example, they give a 10 percent discount to American and Canadian automobile associations.

Days Inn. This chain is directed at clientele with a medium level of purchasing power. This company brand name possesses the greatest number of hotel rooms, with a total of 153,701. The company's slogan, "Follow the Sun," is indicative of the chain's strategy, as it plans to open hotels throughout a large part of the world.

Accor

Accor owns the Ibis, Formule 1, Etap, Motel 6, and Red Roof Inn brand names.

Formule 1 and Etap. These are Accor's most reasonably priced brand names. The company defines Formule 1 as a zero-star hotel, while Etap hotels are considered to be "one-and-a-half" star hotels with a few more services than those offered by Formule 1, although they are still in the lower price range. Etap hotels are moderately priced and vary in architectural style.

Ibis. These hotels offer limited services and are directed at business travelers and tourists. About half the brand name's hotels are located in city centers, strategic and/or tourist areas, or near airports.

Motel 6. This is a chain of roadside motels, most of which are in the United States (with a minor presence in Toronto, Canada, since 1999). It competes directly with brand names such as Travelodge and Days Inn, both of which belong to Cendant Corporation.

Red Roof Inns. This is a chain of U.S. roadside motels, present in thirty-eight states, mostly in the Midwest, East, and South. Its clients are mainly business travelers.

Choice Hotels International

Choice Hotels International owns the brand names Sleep Inn, Rodeway Inn, and Econo Lodge, among others.

Sleep Inns. These are reasonably priced hotels that are refurbished on a regular, mandatory basis. They have rooms with automated systems and limited services, with fourteen employees per 100 rooms.

Rodeway Inns. These are inexpensive hotels with conference rooms, full restaurant service, and a swimming pool. Some rooms are specially adapted for elderly guests.

Econo Lodges. These offer rooms with limited services at reduced rates. They have conference rooms and a swimming pool.

Marriott International

Marriott International has, among others, the following three brand names.

Fairfield Inn. These are one-half–star, reasonably priced hotels offering limited services.

SpringHill Suites. This brand name, which offers a limited number of services, replaced the Fairfield Suite brand name during the last quarter of 1998, incorporating all its hotels (characterized by suite-based accommodation only) that were already in operation or in the process of being built.

TownePlace Suites. This is a reasonably priced product for longer stays. The suites have work areas and emphasis is placed on the hotels' services and homelike comforts and conveniences.

Other Companies Using Cost Leadership Strategy

Hilton Hotel Corporation. Its brand names include Hampton Inns, which offer limited services, and Hampton Inn & Suites, whose hotels offer a combination of traditional hotel rooms and residential-style suites.

InterContinental. Its brand name Express by Holiday is directed at the cheapest end of the market (mainly in the United States). With limited services and facilities, its hotels are reasonably priced and less expensive than Holiday Inns'.

Differentiation Strategy

Marriott International

Marriott International has the Ritz-Carlton brand name, directed at the luxury segment of the market. Although J.W. Marriott Hotels might be regarded as being in the same category, Ritz-Carlton hotels tend to be deluxe properties that are a cut above Marriott International. Most operate under the name Ritz-Carlton, although some have their own individual names.

Starwood Hotels & Resorts Worldwide

Starwood Hotels & Resorts Worldwide operates a brand name called The Luxury Collection/St. Regis. Launched in January 1995 as "The Luxury Collection," this brand name is still lacking in definition. The name, which sounds more like a description than a trademark, is used by some Ciga and Sheraton hotels.

Four Seasons

Four Seasons, with its two brand names, Four Seasons and Regent, is positioned at the top of the international hotel industry's highest segment. Executives aim for each hotel to be the local market leader. Four Seasons' existing inner-city hotels and those under construction are located in some of the top commercial and business centers, which normally have easy access to tourist attractions.

Hyatt

Hyatt's deluxe Grand Hyatt brand name is also based on the differentiation strategy. This brand serves large business destinations, and large-scale meetings and conventions. The business hotels include state-of-the-art technology, sophisticated business and leisure facilities, banquet and conference facilities of world-class standard, and specialized programs.

Carlson Hospitality Worldwide

Carlson Hospitality Worldwide has a prestigious brand name called Regent, directed at the luxury end of the market. Since 1970, it has been providing discerning business and leisure travelers with the highest standards of luxury hospitality.

Shangri-La

Shangri-La's Shangri-La Hotels and Resorts are mainly five-star hotels. Its inner-city hotels tend to be bigger than its holiday hotels. Most have over 500 rooms. The name Shangri-La was inspired by James Hilton's legendary novel *Lost Horizon*. A tranquil haven in the mountains of Tibet, Shangri-La wants to be recognized as a synonym for paradise (www.shangri-la.com).

Hilton Hotels Corporation

Hilton Hotels Corporation[7] dedicates its Hilton Hotels brand name to this strategy. These are high-class hotels located in big business centers, leading cities, airports, and tourist resorts in the United States. The brand name's flagships are the Waldorf Astoria, the Hilton Hawaiian Village Beach Resort and Spa, and the Palmer House Hilton.

InterContinental

InterContinental devotes its InterContinental brand name to this strategy. These are five-star, well-established luxury hotels with an excellent reputation worldwide. The newest hotels are large capacity, with an average of 370 rooms (excluding Global Partner Hotels & Resorts), and they are located in the world's largest cities.

Sol Meliá

Sol Meliá's Gran Meliá subbrand name also uses the differentiation strategy. It is aimed at the Meliá's top segment of the market. These hotels are located in the centers of the world's leading cities and in some top tourist resorts.

Market Niche Strategy

Some examples of segments in which the world's leading hotel chains have positioned themselves will now be described.

In the *limited service* segment Accor stands out from the rest with its Ibis brand name; InterContinental with its Express by Holiday Inn brand name; Hilton Hotels Corporation with Hampton Inn; and Marriott International with Fairfield and SpringHill Suites.

In the *roadside tourism* segment, which is so important in the United States, Cendant Corporation holds a position of prime importance with its Super 8, Travelodge, and Knights Inn brand names. Accor is also positioned in the same segment with its Motel 6 brand name.

In the *long-stay* segment, mention should be made of the following chains: Marriott International with TownePlace Suites and Residence Inn; InterContinental with Staybridge Suites; and Choice Hotels International with MainStay Suites (positioned in the mid-to-high segment of the market).

Business travel is catered to by companies such as InterContinental with its Holiday Inn Select brand name, Cendant Corporation with Wingate Inns,[8] and Sol Meliá with its Meliá brand name, composed of four- and five-star hotels.

SUMMARY

An important aspect to bear in mind in an analysis of competitive strategies is the value chain. With it, company leaders should be able to identify what activities they can influence in order to bring about some of the proposed competitive strategies: *cost leadership, differentiation,* and *focus or market niche* strategies.

This chapter focused on why competitive advantages have enabled leading international hotel chains to achieve a key strategic position that allowed them to expand. The greatest growth was experienced by hotel chains that have opted mainly for the cost leadership strategy, such as Cendant Corporation.

Chapter 3

Diversification versus Specialization

THE THEORY

Diversification might be considered one of the main features of the evolution of developed capitalist economies. During recent decades, the incorporation of new activities to a company's existing ones has been considered sufficient, if not almost essential, for its transformation into or continuance as a dynamic business with good future prospects. Thus businesses with a single or dominant activity gave way to ones with multiple activities, whether interrelated or not.

A clearer illustration of the importance of diversification can be found in the pioneering works of Chandler (1962) and Ansoff (1965, 1976). Likewise, a gradual awareness is also discernable in specialist literature of the significance of what the decision to diversify implies. An impressive number of works on the subject are available, even though conclusions continue to be incomplete and controversial (Ramanujan and Varadarajan, 1989). Among these works are studies on the relationship between the type of diversification and company performance, directed at investigating and achieving a better understanding of the (at times hidden) mechanisms of this relationship. These mechanisms are to be found mainly in the structure of the sector with which the diversification-related activities are associated and in the structure of the business and its system of management.

In reality, these in-depth studies of diversification reflect another gradual awareness: the need for serious strategic reflection on the decision to diversify.

One cannot deny the well-known, spectacular success of certain firms whose growth has been based on diversification; however, evidence also exists of a high failure rate. Some authors even consider the search for growth to be one of the main reasons behind a drop in profitability, and for a company to abandon the field of business it knows well in order to diversify is dangerous (Daigne, 1986). Indeed, during the 1980s, greater caution by business leaders could be discerned, and past decisions to diversify were even reconsidered, with a strong tendency to revert to the company's base activities.

Leaders must be very careful in choosing the most suitable form of growth: either a company grows by *specializing* (i.e., intensifying its efforts but continuing to center its resources on the same activity or activities that characterize its present field of business), or it grows by *diversifying* (i.e., dedicating its existing or new resources to a new activity or activities that are different from the existing one(s), thus modifying its field of business). Although this change implies new horizons and the company's increased growth potential, it is not without risks or resistance, so a minimum knowledge of diversification is crucial. This means knowing what diversification represents, knowing when and why to diversify, understanding how to do it, and realizing what implications it will have for the company.

A clearer understanding of the exact nature of diversification can be found by comparing it with an alternative form of growth: specialization.

If, as a starting point, Ansoff's famous growth vector matrix (1976) is accepted, two forms of growth are possible: expansion and diversification. Diversification occurs only when a company attempts to grow by introducing a new product to a new market, i.e., fulfilling a new mission. It therefore means the incorporation of a new product-market pair or of an activity or activities different from the existing one(s). In contrast, expansion is the result of market penetration (intensifying efforts to increase the company's share of its existing products in the existing market), market development (seeking new markets for the company's existing products), or product development (offering new products to the existing markets).

During the development of this new activity additional factors will be involved that hold the keys to success, together with a different competitive environment. This requires knowledge and the development of a new field of business with the resulting need for more skills.

Remember that in response to the demands of a more complex reality Ansoff (1976) perfected his growth vector by situating it in a three-dimensional space. Thus executives can expand their companies by penetrating new geographic markets, meeting new market needs, or introducing new technologies in such a way that multiple strategic combinations and approaches are open to them, from continuing to meet the traditional needs of their usual markets with traditional technology to making an energetic bid to reposition themselves in the three dimensions.

This definition of the nature of diversification helps us to understand that when a company executive decides to diversify, his or her success depends not only on the potential growth and profitability of the new business activity, but also (and above all) on the company's capacity to develop whatever new skills are required for this activity and even for this new field of business. This reveals the expansion- or specialization-related difficulties that diversification entails. Perhaps a company should diversify only when it cannot expand by specialization (Strategor, 1988).

We will now indicate what steps to take before deciding to diversify. In other words, possible different *ways* of specializing will be discussed.

The first way, as already mentioned, is to penetrate the current market, meeting the same needs with the same technology. Should no growth potential exist in market penetration, a second alternative can be considered: geographical expansion. This includes a search for new markets, even those of other countries (i.e., taking into account the possibility of internationalization). In this case internationalization is the result of a specialization strategy,[1] even though at times entering other countries is considered a form of *international diversification* (Rochet, 1981). A highly different environment can call for new skills and this, as previously mentioned, is characteristic of diversification.

The third method of specialization partly includes what is known as *marketing diversification.* This type of diversification, which we will classify as specialization in certain cases provided that it does not require new business skills, includes strategies such as offering complementary products (new needs); searching for new clients with the same needs whose requirements we will meet with the same technology; and even developing products to replace or substitute for the existing ones (new technology).

These three types of marketing diversification can be considered forms of specialization only if some kind of additional skill is not needed. This case is most typical when trying to extend the services a company offers its traditional clients through complementary products that permit the extension of the business activity's growth phase. It is less usual for this to occur when the products have new clients, as this might require or even necessitate a new key to success and, therefore, a new skill. Last, maintaining the same type of know-how when substitute products are involved is difficult, as they tend to be developed with new technology.

This third form of specialization is ambiguous. The need for new skills that will extend and/or prolong the company's growth potential in a certain field of business cannot always be anticipated, particularly, as is the case here, if it is not a question of penetrating a totally different activity. Thus company leaders must be ready to cross this somewhat vague frontier between specialization and diversification without actually having anticipated doing so.

The warning just made is based on the inherent nature of diversification because if a company leader cannot unite the resources, abilities, and, in global terms, skills needed for a new activity, the company's possibilities of success in this field of business will be heavily compromised and, consequently, so will its growth strategy. Also, if the problem is not discovered in time, the entire company may be endangered.

A large number of company executives have abandoned certain activities over the past few years in order to refocus their attention on what they consider to be their key (and perhaps traditional) activity or activities as part of the restructurization of their global business activities. This phenomenon, which should not go ignored, might be interpreted as a consequence of the new economic framework. Business owners dealt with crisis-related problems by avoiding the dispersal of additional resources and, at the same time, by focusing their efforts on a few limited activities in order to achieve a critical mass. This trend continues to increase in popularity among certain sectors in the process of globalization.

Nevertheless, this phenomenon might also signify the recognition that diversification is a luxury reserved for thriving companies and that simultaneous diversification and specialization strategies require a large number of resources and skills of all types (Strategor, 1988).

As a general rule, it is better for a company to center all its resources and efforts on one activity while some possibility of development exists and a better, stronger market position can be achieved. However, other good reasons may prompt a company leader to adopt a diversification strategy, even when the growth potential offered by specialization has not been exhausted, as will be discussed later.

This definition of diversification is incomplete without mentioning one of its fundamental characteristics: *synergies*. They are not only a characteristic of the definition so far given, but also a consequence. A synergy can be described as the effect produced by a combination of several different elements as compared with the separate effects of each individual element.

Diversification means becoming involved in a new activity and, therefore, acquiring and developing a set of specific skills for that activity. Obviously, a company ought not to diversify if it does not have at least some of the necessary skills for the new activity. The type of diversification and business activity that a company executive chooses is heavily dependent on the existence of synergies between the company's own skills and those required by the new activity.

Among a company's different functions, certain resources and skills may be underused by the existing activities (e.g., production facilities, research teams, and staff with specific training). They could, however, be dedicated to other activities (e.g., technology, distribution channels, brand names) without restricting the company's business capacity. Reusing these resources or skills by dedicating them to other activities will increase their degree of productivity. Furthermore, if a company has a skill that can also be shared by a new activity, the company has an initial competitive advantage in this field of business. In some cases, diversification can even be a consequence of improving how company skills are used.

When diversifying, the more synergies a company tries to take advantage of, the more possibilities of success it will have. However, these are only potential synergies; management must try to make them real. It is relatively unusual for only one type of synergy to be produced during diversification, although a company may seek to produce one main synergy.

There are two major types of diversification: *concentric* and conglomerate. The first type can also be divided into two different forms.

Concentric or *homogenous* diversification can be defined as the incorporation of new business activities that are either technically or commercially associated with the company's existing ones, in order to try to produce one of the aforementioned synergies.

Within the field of concentric diversification, a form known as *horizontal* diversification can be distinguished. According to Ansoff (1965), horizontal diversification is characterized by a similarity between the company's new clients and its current ones, together with the use of the same distribution channels. Often it is a question of similar products/markets, although a new identity is used (Rochet, 1981). *Vertical* diversification or vertical integration means that the company becomes involved in activities from other levels of the production chain, either by moving backward, so that the company integrates the activity of one of its suppliers, or forward, so that it integrates the activity of one of its clients.

Conglomerate (or *pure* or *heterogeneous*) diversification is characterized by a total absence of any relation between the new activities and the ones existing before diversification. This does not, however, preclude a synergy, as this type of diversification normally involves the search for a financial synergy. It is an extreme way of practicing the logic of the business portfolio (Durán, 1977). Often a synergy is based on management skills. Diversification founded on management skills is a privileged technique used by numerous American conglomerates, based on recognition of management's universal nature and its crucial importance.

As already stated, different reasons exist for introducing a diversification strategy. Identifying the reason to diversify is as necessary as understanding the nature of diversification if a minimum chance of success is to be guaranteed.

Generally speaking, diversification allows a company to maintain a growth strategy by conquering new positions and new profit areas. In this case, diversification could be considered an offensive tactic, introduced for proactive reasons. However, diversification can also be a defensive measure and, consequently, the logic behind it can vary more than one might initially think.

Thus the main reasons that lead to diversification are

- the need to invest a surplus of money or skill,
- risk reduction,
- an attempt to strengthen the firm's competitive position, and
- the need to revitalize the company's portfolio of activities.

The logic behind diversification ranges from a clearly offensive strategy (when taking advantage of financial or other surplus resources) to a wholly defensive tactic (i.e., diversification for survival), passing through what could be considered intermediate examples of an offensive-defensive strategy. When the reason for diversification is to reduce the firm's global risks, reinforce its competitive position, or attempt to revitalize it, the importance of each type of logic will vary according to the case in question.

As well as bearing in mind the reason why one wishes to diversify, the type of diversification will also influence the choice of activity or activities to be included in the company's portfolio. The degree of similarity or coincidence between the company's current skills and the skills and key factors needed for potential new activities all acquire a very special relevance.

However, this search for the greatest possible synergy might be indicative of a conservative attitude. Indeed, it might even hinder the search for an effective solution to the growth, risk, or even survival problem, since preferred activities tend to be closely linked commercially or technically to the existing ones. Consequently, when identifying potential areas for diversification and choosing the best possible activity or activities, the initial requirements are imagination and creativity, followed by a dose of realism.

If, as is clearly possible, a company decides to diversify not because an opportunity exists, but due to one of the problems mentioned in the analysis of the different reasons behind diversification, a wide range of potential new activities should be proposed, depending on the goals to be achieved. These, in turn, are dependent on the logic behind the decision to diversify, which should have been clearly defined. Available techniques can assist in the search for diversified activities.

Regarding realism, leaders must be aware of the efforts required, in terms of company skills, to develop the chosen activity so as to ensure success (in other words, deciding whether the company is capable of making these efforts). Furthermore, leaders must determine what the firm's minimum competitive status would be, below which diversification would bring more problems than solutions for the company. Indeed experience seems to confirm that profitable examples of diversification are cases in which businesses become involved in a new activity and concentrate their resources in order to achieve a critical mass. Biggadike (1979) demonstrates that at a midpoint of about seven or eight years diversified activities should start to show satisfactory returns, although this period can be considerably reduced if the company makes a "massive entry" into its chosen area of business. Many diversified companies have needed to "recenter" themselves because this critical mass has sometimes not been reached.

The last issue to discuss in the adoption of a diversification strategy is the possible organizational problems that diversification might cause. The benefits of diversification are not automatic, and part of the risk of a failed diversification strategy is the potential organizational resistance and problems that it can generate.

Numerous studies have been made of the relationship between companies' general organizational structure and growth, and specific diversification strategies. A company's divisional structure supports its diversification strategy, since it provides flexibility and autonomy, both of which are necessary given the diversity that diversification implies.

Remember, though, that one of the crucial aspects of diversification is the ability to take advantage of synergies. This could be hindered by the excessive independence of a company's different divisions and activities, thereby compromising the success of the diversification strategy. Good coordination is therefore another organizational factor to consider.

Mention also tends to be made of the possible increased fragility of diversified companies in times of crisis. It is virtually impossible to centralize decision making (a measure that a survival strategy often demands, for example), and top executives cannot ensure their familiarity with and ability to control different aspects of activities that are often extremely different from one another (above all in the case of highly diversified and/or conglomerate businesses).

In addition to a company's organizational structure, other factors are essential in the correct application of a diversification strategy, such as information, communication, leadership, and an appropriate business culture.

A diversification strategy's chance of success will increase if the firm's leaders are able to involve all members of management (including their top executives, intermediate managers, and even employees), making them aware of the need to diversify and therefore allowing them to share their vision of the company's future. This is a very important communicative task, and it should not stop once the new activity has commenced. Instead, it should continue with the diffusion of the company's initial results and further expectations, among other things, so as to increase people's motivation and to continue encouraging creativity.

Nevertheless, a feeling of involvement will not be achieved without an adequate incentive system and style of leadership, or without the ad hoc, prior training of the management team and staff involved in the new activity. Internal communication and, more particularly, the creation of transversal groups (made up of people involved in existing and new activities) are also good methods of integration. For example, the "management-rotation" system is considered a reliable, necessary form of conduct by most international diversified companies that achieve high performance levels (Calori and Harvatopoulos, 1988). With this last system, not only is mobility an interesting way to integrate activities, but it also underlies the importance of the company's business culture (which is, in turn, a condition of integration and a possible source of organizational resistance).

This is why, with a diversification strategy, the coexistence of a common cultural core is recommended, with features and cultural practices adapted to each of the corresponding activities, depending on the peculiarities of its related environment. For example, this common core could be an ongoing search for product and management quality, or human relations based on responsibility and initiatives (Calori and Harvatopoulos, 1988). Consequently, a certain compatibility must be present between the company's identity and its chosen form of diversification. Nevertheless, the cultural barriers that are sometimes raised during a diversification strategy are not always directly attributable to diversification itself, but to the way in which it is done, i.e., by a takeover or joint venture. Internationalization tends to make this kind of problem more acute.

The decision to diversify must be the result of strategic reflection, allowing the leaders to clarify why and how to do it. A careful choice must be made about the type of diversification, the new activity, and the best method of introducing it, taking into account the characteristics of the company and its environment. Likewise, the implications of the strategic change that diversification always implies must be analyzed and understood from the perspective of the company's organizational structure, systems (information, administrative procedures, motivation, etc.), management style, and organizational culture.

Here again is the concept of an inherent management balance and, in particular, an inherent strategic management balance between the formulation and application of the strategy, between what the strategy must consist of and what it could consist of. This concept is perfectly expressed in a sentence by Drucker (1975) in which, when faced with the decision to diversify, he highlights the need to ask oneself the following questions: What is the lowest form of diversification the company could undergo in order to achieve its objectives and still continue to be a stable, profitable business, able to compete successfully with its rivals? What is the greatest degree of diversification the company could tolerate, given the additional complexity that it generates?

Having analyzed the theoretical problems of diversification, we will now study examples from the world's leading hotel chains. Cendant Corporation, InterContinental, Accor, Marriott International, and Carlson Hospitality Worldwide have all developed clear diversification strategies, while in practical terms Choice Hotels International, Sol Meliá, and, more recently, Hilton Hotels Corporation and Starwood Hotels & Resorts Worldwide have opted for the specialization strategy.

EXAMPLES

Diversification Strategy

Cendant Corporation

Cendant Corporation[2] ranks first among the world's hotel chains and is one of the companies that has undergone significant growth in this field. However, the group is not dedicated only to the hotel business. It has three very different divisions, mainly focused on three different business areas: hotels and travel, real estate, and marketing alliances. The *hotel and travel* division offers clients all kinds of services that are characteristic of this sector, including travel and hotel bookings, car rentals, and time-share services.

In 1999, Cendant Corporation bought the entire share capital of the Avis car rental firm for 930 million dollars. Avis is now the world's second largest car rental franchise company.[3] It has a fleet of over 200,000 vehicles, with 4,900 offices and over 18,000 workers. Avis's main U.S. competitors are Hertz Corporation and National Car Rental.

In 2000, a joint venture was started between AVIS Group and PHH Arval. PHH is now the second biggest company in the United States in its specialist field. Its subsidiary, PHH Management Services PLC,[4] leads the field in the United Kingdom. The firm has over one million vehicles and approximately 1,300 employees, meeting the needs of over 500 clients worldwide.

Finally, Capital Logistics is a bus company whose services include the transportation of airline crews, U.S. bus routes, bus services for hotel companies (transfers to and from airports), and the rental and repair of buses.

Cendant Group also has a vacation exchange service, run by Resort Condominium International (RCI), a company that it acquired on November 12, 1996. Founded in 1974, RCI has over 3,900 employees and its own travel agency, RCI Travel, which obtains discounts on flights, cruises, car rentals, etc. At present RCI has a portfolio of over 3 million time-share owners and more than 3,700 time-share properties in over 100 countries.[5]

Cendant Corporation extended the time-share properties it handles by buying Fairfield Communities for 635 million dollars. This is the biggest time-share chain in the United States, with over 324,000 accommodation units.

The *real estate* division is organized into the following business operations: franchises for real estate agencies, relocation services, and consumer mortgage services.

Cendant Corporation is the world's leading franchiser of real estate agencies. The company runs this division under the Century 21,

Coldwell Banker, Coldwell Banker Commercial, and ERA brand names.

Cendant Corporation entered the real estate business following the 1995 purchase of Century 21, now the world's largest name in franchising operations[6] with more than 7,200 franchisee real estate agencies and about 131,800 sales agents. In February 1996 the company bought another franchiser, ERA, consisting of over 2,600 real estate agencies and more than 33,200 sales agents. In May of the same year, Cendant Corporation took over the Coldwell Banker Corporation brand name. This is currently the third most important franchise business, with about 3,650 real estate agencies and 119,800 sales agents. Finally, in 1997 Cendant purchased NRT Incorporated to merge it with the other brand names from the sector that the company owned. As a result of this merger, NRT is now Cendant Corporation's biggest franchiser, with more than 12,000 franchisee offices. Cendant Corporation's main business rivals are Prudential, Better Homes and Gardens, and RE/MAX.

The company runs its relocation services through the Cendant Mobility Services brand name. This is currently one of the most important relocation companies in the United States, accounting for the relocation of over 100,000 people per year.[7] Cendant Mobility Services has some 2,200 employees in 111 countries. It offers a full range of services for company employees who are forced to relocate, including moving services (65,000 moves per year), the search for and purchase of a new home, and information on the cost of living in the new location.

The company's mortgage business is run by Cendant Mortgage, which offers mortgage services to clients buying a new home. The company, with more than 7,000 employees, now operates throughout the entire United States.

By entering into a number of *marketing alliances*, Cendant Corporation has created over twenty programs of goods and services to cover virtually all of its clients' needs.

Despite the fact that until very recently Cendant Corporation's different companies each operated independently, and although it does not have any airlines or travel agents of its own, enormous potential exists within the group for the development of synergies. This company is less well equipped, in some ways, than Carlson Hospitality Worldwide and Accor, which share the ownership of one of the world's three most important travel agent groups, Carlson Wagonlit, as well as possessing a wide range of hotel brand names. Nevertheless, Cendant Corporation's access to direct marketing programs reduces its need for another hotel demand producer.

InterContinental

InterContinental is the biggest hotel chain in the world. Like Cendant Corporation, it is not dedicated exclusively to the hotel business, because it is also active in two other very important sectors: the complementary leisure services industry and the soft drinks industry (Britvic Soft Drinks).

The *complementary leisure services* managed by InterContinental include over 3,000 different businesses. This is one of the most important companies in the industry, with approximately 50,000 employees. The company was formed when InterContinental underwent a restructuring process in the early 1990s, consisting of the sale of those businesses that were no longer profitable for the company such as amusement arcades, bingo halls, and betting shops, and the regrouping of businesses under the same management team. This led to the creation of the Mitchells and Butlers division, with three well-defined business areas: bars, pubs, and restaurants.

In September 1995, Mitchells and Butlers purchased 127 Harvester restaurants, and it now has 130 of them. It currently owns thirty-nine Toby Carvery restaurants, which were initially opened in southern England and are now among the market's world leaders. It also owns 151 Vintage Inns and has seventy pubs in Ireland operating under the name O'Neill's. It also owns fifty-four All Bar Ones, ninety It's a Creams, and twenty-one Hollywood Bowls, in addition to twenty-six Edwars.

In 2001, Mitchells and Butlers added new brand names to its division of pubs and restaurants, including Arena, Emberinns, Flares, Goose, Sizzling, Browns, Aex, and Inn Keeper's Lodge.

Its *soft drinks* business is run by Britvic Soft Drinks, a very important soft drink producer in the United Kingdom. It makes fifteen leading brands of drink, producing 1,100 million liters of soft drinks each year with a turnover of 539 million pounds. It includes the brand names Pepsi, Robinsons, and Tango.

Accor

Accor is the fourth biggest hotel chain in the world and, like the two previous ones, it has also adopted a diversification strategy. More specifically, the French company is involved in the travel agency sector as a wholesaler and retailer (something that will be analyzed in more detail in Chapter 4, "Vertical Integration").

Accor has an Accor Corporate Services division, which oversees the different services offered by the company.[8] Accor's services are organized into three product segments:

1. *Meeting Live Essentials.* Specific solutions, allowing companies to subcontract several different services, for example, "Ticket Car" and "Ticket Combustible" (service stations), "Clean Way" (launderers of work clothes), and "Supreme Award" and "Top Premium" (gift vouchers), so companies can reward employees for increased productivity, quality, sales, etc. Via its coordination platform, Accor Incentive Network, Accor offers clients motivation and incentive programs, as well as global or tailor-made options.

2. *Enhancing Well-Being.* Personalized assistance for employees and companies (Childcare Vouchers, Familylife Solutions). In some countries Accor has launched products that offer users access to health services. One example is its Eyecare Vouchers in the United Kingdom, Germany, and Sweden.

3. *Improving Performance.* For restaurants, supermarkets, and other affiliates. There are three types of products: "RestauShop" (for the purchase of food and other goods), "RestauPratic" (restaurant management), and "RestauPlanet" (Internet reservations and customer care). By the year 2002, the group had invested a total of 100 million euros in its continued technological development.

Marriott International

The Marriott International hotel chain is listed on the New York, Chicago, Philadelphia, and Pacific stock markets. It was created in 1993 when Marriott Corporation divided into two separate companies. Marriott Corporation was renamed Host Marriott Corporation and took charge of the hotel real estate business, and Marriott International became responsible for hotel management and its service business. Marriott International, a worldwide accommodation service, operates in the United States and in sixty-four other countries. The company, with headquarters in Washington, DC, employs a workforce of about 133,000 people.

Marriott International is engaged in the time-share business through its Marriott Vacation Club International division and its Horizons, Grand Residence, and Ritz-Carlton Club brand names. The division currently has over 6,900 time-share properties.

The division did not have a very strong presence, but executives hope that the increasing importance of the time-share business, particularly in Spain, will contribute toward the division's development. The following factors will strengthen this division:

- New legislation establishes a framework for development and action that inspires greater confidence and security; this is beneficial for both the promoter and the consumer. A trend toward the increasing regulation of the time-share sector is occurring, and the European Union may enact a second directive on time-sharing.
- The hotel trade's integration of time-share activities has played a key role in helping to develop the time-share concept, and it will continue to do so. Time-share's inclusion in the business activities of big hotel chains gives it an image of seriousness and reliability that increases clients' confidence. Examples of international hotel chains involved in the time-share business are Hyatt, Hilton Hotels Corporation, Starwood Hotels & Resorts, Four Seasons, Marriott International, Grupo Posadas, Pestana, and Disney. Spanish hotel chains include Sol Meliá, Occidental (through its Allegro brand name), Barceló, Confortel, Hesperia, and Hotetur.
- At present one can also buy time-share vacations on catamarans in the Caribbean, in houseboats on the English canals, or in recreational vehicle (RV) parks. These examples show that the industry is going through a process of diversification, from the perspective of products and commercialization, so as to adapt to new times and new consumer profiles and requirements.

- The time-share industry's sales have multiplied by 1,000 in the past twenty-five years, and at present the segment is growing at a rate of between 8 and 10 percent per year, while the tourist sector in general is growing at a rate of 3 to 4 percent per year.
- Efforts are clearly being made to improve the quality offered by the time-share industry, as this is one of the subsectors of the tourist industry to have requested its inclusion in the PICTE (the Spanish Integral Plan for Tourism Quality). The image of the time-share business and its quality standards will continue to improve.

These factors have recently led Marriott International's time-share division to invest in Spain. Its investments include the inauguration of the Marriott Golf Resort & Spa in Majorca.

Finally, the company also has several amusement parks and a cruise line that travels around the Caribbean and Mediterranean seas.

Carlson Hospitality Worldwide

Carlson Hospitality Worldwide has adopted what is essentially a strategy of vertical diversification (also known as vertical integration), like the French hotel chain Accor. Consequently, its problems will also be analyzed in Chapter 4, "Vertical Integration." In addition to its strategy of vertical integration, the U.S. chain is also a major presence in the restaurant business, with 746 restaurants in fifty-three countries, and a total of 74,600 employees. Five hundred seventy-six of its restaurants are located in the United States and 170 are distributed throughout the rest of the world. Carlson Restaurants has 746 restaurants franchised and licensed. They are operated under the brands of Friday's (with a total of 671 restaurants under the brand names T.G.I. Friday's, Front Row Sports Grill, and American Bar, it runs 232 of these itself and 439 are franchises) and Pick Up Stix (with a total of fifty-three restaurants, it owns forty-nine of these outright and the other four are franchise operations). Last, it has full ownership of a series of U.S. brand names including FISHBOWL, Italianni's, Mignon, Timpano Italian Chophouse, Samba Room, Star Canyon, and Taqueria Canonita, together totaling twenty-two restaurants.

Specialization Strategy

Hilton Hotels Corporation is a "pure" hotel chain, as its entertainment division separated from Hilton Hotels in 1998, with the creation of Park Place, which is also listed on the New York Stock Exchange. Hilton Hotels Corporation leaders are hotel operators in the widest sense of the word, as they develop, own, run, and offer franchises for hotels, vacation complexes, and time-share complexes in the United States and in other countries.

In 1996, when Steven Bollenbach was named company chairman,[9] Hilton Hotels Corporation moved into the gaming market for the first time, with the purchase of Bally Entertainment Corporation for 3.1 billion dollars.[10] This gave it a strong position in Atlantic City (the second biggest casino town in the United States after Las Vegas) and increased the number of the properties it owned in Las Vegas. However, just two years later, Hilton Hotels Corporation sold its casinos to Park Place Entertainment to counteract a possible drop in the price of Hilton Hotels Corporation's shares, caused by the uncertain future of the gaming industry. At the same time, once separate, its hotel business would have more flexibility, enabling it to merge with another company from the hotel industry.

Starwood Hotels & Resorts Worldwide is a pure hotel chain, meaning that their only business is the hotel trade. The company was also involved in the gaming business before the sale of Caesars to Park Place Entertainment. In 2000, Starwood Hotels & Resorts Worldwide acquired Vistana, thereby entering the time-share business. Choice Hotels International and Sol Meliá are also pure hotel chains.

During the past few years, the hotel industry has followed one of two paths: a split from leisure conglomerates to create companies that focus more heavily on the hotel business or, in a parallel but contradictory move, diversification in order to take advantage of the strength and solidity of certain brand names.

The conglomerates' separation has been more dramatic in the United States and in Europe. In the United States, both Starwood Hotels & Resorts Worldwide and Hilton Hotels Corporation left the casino business, selling Caesars and Bally Entertainment Corporation to Park Place Entertainment.

In the United Kingdom, all the leisure companies listed on the stock market have undergone considerable changes. Whitbread and InterContinental abandoned the beer industry and the pub business after centuries of being associated with the alcoholic drinks trade. Hilton Group PLC is Ladbrokes' new name, after executives decided to sell their casinos and concentrate on hotels for business travelers. Rank Group has sold most of its businesses, including its holiday division, and Granada is now a media company, after owners sold their hotels to Compass.

Mainland Europe and Asia have also experienced this obsession with breakaways. Accor, for example, sold the car rental firm Europcar to Volkswagen, and some Asian conglomerates have sold their hotels. Raffles Holdings was launched on the Singapore Stock Exchange as a hotel company, splitting from the other interests of its parent company.

In a move that seems to contradict the trend for businesses to separate, some companies have extended their brand names to encompass other new areas. The time-share business has become a popular way of extending a brand name's activities. Although it used to be synonymous with shady sales techniques, the time-share business underwent a change of image in the 1990s. For this reason, a number of prestigious brand names have shown an interest, such as Marriott, Disney, Hyatt, Hilton, and Four Seasons.

Cendant Corporation, Marriott International, Starwood Hotels & Resorts Worldwide, and Hilton Hotels Corporation are the four chains from the Top 10 hotel chains with the greatest number of rooms that have entered the time-share business with the most enthusiasm. This is mainly attributable to four factors:

1. The strong growth that this market has experienced in recent years, as it currently accounts for a turnover of over 5 billion dollars in the United States, equivalent to the Spanish hotel industry's total turnover, and the good short-term prospects
2. The high purchasing power of time-share clients, whose approximate income per family exceeds 65,000 dollars
3. The fact that, generally speaking, time-share clients are more frequent than hotel guests, as they take about two vacations per year and two short breaks
4. The high degree of time-share client loyalty

The first hotel business to move into the time-share sector was Marriott, which bought American Resorts in 1984. Marriott Vacation Club International had the highest time-share sales in the world in 1999. Nearly 25 percent of its sales are estimated to be the result of links with other Marriott business activities, particularly its hotels. Cendant Corporation is another big time-share competitor, with the largest exchange business: RCI. At the end of 2000, owners also bought the vacation promoter Fairfield Communities to position Cendant in all areas of the business.

Another form of expansion that Marriott International pioneered was its move into the business of senior living centers. Marriott International created its Senior Living Services in 1984 and opened over 150 homes.[11] The basic services offered by its senior living centers range from separate home-style apartments to full medical care. Due to the aging of the population in general, this market offers a very strong potential source of income for big hotel groups.

Another industry that has attracted companies is the cruise line business. Carlson executives used their Radisson brand name to create Radisson Seven Seas Cruises. The American multinational is considered to be the world's biggest supplier of luxury cruises. Similarly, Club Med[12] offers a range of unconventional hotels, including cruise ships and vacation villas. It is also seeking to extend its brand name's coverage to include lifestyle operations, such as nightclubs.

The biggest example of brand name expansion might well be the move by tour operators into the hotel business. This vertical integration has been particularly significant in Europe, with examples such as TUI GROUP, Airtours, and C&N Touristic. These are very big operations that will be analyzed in greater detail in the next chapter.

SUMMARY

Growth decisions are associated with a company's business strategy and affect the company as a whole by redefining its field of activity. As a result, expansion is virtually a "must" for businesses in a modern, dynamic economy. Thus if company leaders decide to expand, the next step is to analyze all the possible growth opportunities. That is, they should consider in which direction they wish to expand in order to define growth activity. This means contemplating two possible alternatives: specialization or diversification. In this chapter, we analyzed and contrasted both forms of expansion, examining key factors such as what the two strategies entail, possible motives, methods, and synergies, as well as the organizational problems that diversification can involve. Finally, we examined ways in which the world's biggest hotel chains have applied these strategies, examining whether they opted for diversification (into another field of activity or into other sectors of the tourist industry) or specialization. Outstanding examples are Cendant Corporation and Hilton Hotels Corporation. The former is a prime example of a diversified tourism conglomerate (through its travel, hotel, and real estate divisions and its marketing alliances), while the latter specializes in the hotel trade.

Chapter 4

Vertical Integration

THE THEORY

Vertical integration is the oldest system of organizing a company financially, as it is the basic principle of a survival economy. A company that is fully vertically integrated carries out all the activities involved in the different levels of the production chain of a specific type of goods, from providing raw materials to delivering the finished product to the consumer. Nevertheless, when economists study vertical integration, they logically base their studies on the industrial structures derived from the industrial revolution and mass production, where mechanization and specialization in fact led to the vertical disintegration of economic processes (Chandler, 1987).

Many companies, from the late nineteenth century onward, have followed a strategy of vertical integration. A great deal of reading matter on the subject can be found, particularly in the field of industrial economy.[1] Although arguments in favor of vertical integration can be extracted from any number of serious theoretical and empirical studies, from today's perspective these studies have certain limitations that may partially invalidate such positions.

The classic reasons for vertical integration are the search for cost advantages (so that integrated companies can increase their returns) and/or the search for strategic advantages (enabling them to improve their position in relation to their rivals).

Vertical integration generates cost advantages of several kinds by

- encouraging the emergence of economies of scale,
- reducing intermediate stocks,
- limiting control and coordination costs,
- suppressing transaction costs,

- making savings with the elimination of intermediaries' profit margins,
- increasing the efficiency of certain activities, and
- simplifying the production process.

All the reasons just outlined are directed at reducing costs and, therefore, improving the company's overall returns. Is vertical integration heavily based on increased profitability? For a long time this has been believed. The theoretical arguments are substantiated by numerous empirical studies that have demonstrated the economic and financial benefits of vertical integration.

However, most of these studies dealt with large North American companies whose leaders decided to integrate vertically quite a long time before the crisis, during the "golden years" of economic growth.

Today the influence of vertical integration on profitability does not seem so clear, at least not in the expected sense. The conclusions of a number of studies carried out over the past few decades are, at best, eclectic. Some confirm vertical integration's significant impact on profitability, although this impact may be positive or negative depending on the case in question. Others observe that vertical integration does not lead to additional profitability and can even reduce it in the long term. Finally, the famous study on diversification, by Rumelt (1974), highlights the negative results of vertically integrated companies, partially attributing this to drawbacks that will be addressed here later. Harrigan (1983) points out that several research studies based on Profit Impact of Market Strategy (PIMS) data reveal a slight advantage to being more vertically integrated than one's rivals.

Certain strategic reasons can lead to a company's improved competitiveness, based on advantages that are associated with neither lower costs nor higher profitability.

A company's increased market power in comparison with rivals that are not integrated (or the opportunity to bring its position in line with rivals that are already integrated) and improved bargaining power over suppliers and/or clients (if it is not a case of 100 percent integration) are classic arguments put forward by economists to support vertical integration from a company perspective, and to criticize it from the viewpoint of a defense of free market competition. This is because vertical integration creates big entry barriers in industry, closing markets to companies that are not integrated and facilitating possible price discrimination (Harrigan, 1983).

However, this increase in a company's power is sometimes not so straightforward. For example, backward vertical integration, by means of a takeover, can hinder the new activity's development, as the supplier may lose clients, who instead become potential new rivals. If integration takes the form of internal growth, different problems can arise. If a company is not totally self-sufficient in intermediate product supplies, managers will need to continue using other suppliers, which will have become rivals in this new field of business, leading to a possible worsening of relations. Alternatively, if this new activity is run efficiently, the intermediate product's output may be greater than the firm's requirements, meaning that leaders must sell the surplus goods to rivals from its traditional field of business, with all the problems that this implies (Jarillo, 1990). Therefore, when vertical integration is said to represent greater market power, bear in mind the greater complexity and volatility of competitive relationships with current rivals, suppliers, and/or clients.

Another traditional argument in favor of vertical integration is that it gives a company access to certain sources of supplies or certain outlets for its products and/or services. Thus the problems that normally arise due to deadlines, prices, regular supplies, quality, etc., can be removed. In a wider sense, with vertical integration, executives can improve their capacity to anticipate changes in costs or demand, thereby limiting the uncertainty that all business activities are subject to.

Following this line of thought, vertical integration can be used as a backup quality control strategy. Backward vertical integration, for instance, ensures improved, more efficient control of the quality of basic components and, therefore, of the final quality of the company's products or services, an issue that sometimes determines a company's image. With forward vertical integration a company's employees can give end consumers a degree of service and customer care that is more coherent with the company's overall image of quality. In other words, managers could have better control and supervision of the various factors involved in a quality control policy, provided that the integrated company has an organizational structure that ensures more efficient control of divisions and/or departments than it could otherwise exercise over its suppliers or distributors. This is not always so obvious, because it is sometimes easier to replace a supplier or distributor that fails to comply with the company's quality requirements than a division, department, or section that is unable to meet the desired level of quality due to a lack of technical, material, or human resources.

A firm's leaders may also decide to integrate vertically if employees possess and use the latest technology in comparison with their rivals, allowing them to manufacture certain highly specific components, for example, that require state-of-the-art technology. In this case, a sufficiently good reason for integration might be to keep this technological know-how in house rather than give it to suppliers. This argument partly corresponds to the economic transaction cost theory.[2]

Thus vertical integration can offer companies many different opportunities to improve their ability to compete. The expression "opportunity to improve" is used because vertical integration does not automatically imply lower costs, greater quality, etc. Vertical integration simply facilitates certain circumstances that are more conducive to the development of specific strategic company advantages.

However, vertical integration is not completely without danger for companies. The economic, financial, and strategic advantages of vertical integration can be invalidated either partly or entirely with additional detrimental effects if company managers are not able to acquire the necessary new skills when they modify their field of business, or if they are incapable of making the necessary changes to the structure, management systems, and business culture.

This observation is applicable to diversification in general, so it also applies, more specifically, to vertical integration. Equally valid in both cases is the need to consider organizational problems, but they tend to occur more emphatically in the case of vertical integration.

Sometimes a firm's leaders' organizational response to a diversification strategy is to introduce a new divisional structure that provides sufficient autonomy and flexibility for the efficient development of the new business activities. This need for restructurization is rarely acknowledged by companies that integrate vertically, and they seem to continue to give preference to a functional structure, considering that the new activities are somehow subsidiary. As a result, these activities are put under the control of functional services. Moreover, if integration takes the form of external growth, the problem can be aggravated due to conflicts of authority, different business cultures, etc. Nevertheless, this potential problem can be avoided by taking a correct approach to vertical integration and considering it a form of diversification strategy.

Thus the main danger of vertical integration is a loss of flexibility, and this, in turn, is the main reason for vertical integration's loss of prestige and for the increasing popularity of "vertical disintegration." This potential loss of flexibility can take several different forms.

Both backward and forward vertical integration involve modifications to a company's cost structure, with greater emphasis on fixed costs. However, when times are bad, having a cost structure with a high percentage of variable costs is better. Clearly the potential cost of abandoning a supplier or client when there is a big decrease in the demand for a product is normally much lower than underutilizing production or distribution systems. The greater the investment needed for vertical integration and the more specialized this investment is, the more inflexibility this operation will lead to. In the absence of an unfavorable economic climate, the negative repercussions of this reduced flexibility can be detected when newly integrated activities simply do not progress as efficiently as expected, or when stocks can be bought at a lower cost.

The company's greatest overall risk is also associated with its reduced flexibility, as vertical integration implies focusing the risk on a single sector (even though the activities of the production chain's different levels might correspond to different, yet very closely related sectors). If a company's base activity experiences a recession, the entire chain (or almost all of it) may be affected, leading to a buildup of higher costs and even losses in certain phases that the company has integrated.

In an environment characterized by the frequency and speed of technological change, with greater evolution in consumer tastes and demands and a certain tendency toward a search for products that are different from the rest, flexibility is a necessary requirement for a company. Given this framework, vertically integrated companies may seem to be "dinosaurs" in the process of extinction because they have a certain inability to respond rapidly to change, resisting product and process innovations that might lead to disturbances in different levels of the production chain.

Consequently, vertical disintegration could seem to be more sensible (perhaps as a preventive measure). This consists of reducing the company's scope of activity to a few limited activities or levels of the production chain by reestablishing relations with suppliers and/or distributors and postsales services, or by subcontracting companies that are generally smaller, so that they become responsible for activities that the company does not regard as being profitable. This leads to a broader subject, cooperation, which will be dealt with in a subsequent chapter.

This criticism of vertical integration does not mean that leaders of companies that are not vertically integrated should avoid the temptation to integrate because, although it occasionally worked spectacularly in the past, at present it would lead to almost certain failure. Neither do we mean that leaders of integrated companies who wish to preserve their organization must necessarily resort to vertical disintegration.

The changes that have taken place in the business world make vertical integration obsolete, but the old image of vertical integration, in the sense of physically interconnected operations that are 100 percent owned by the company and cover all of its needs, is out of date (Harrigan, 1983).

According to Harrigan, no single form of integration strategy exists. Instead its design is dependent on four different variables:

1. breadth, i.e., technologically different activities that are integrated by the company;
2. the number of phases in the production chain that are covered by each different activity;
3. each activity's degree of internal integration, which may differ and need not necessarily involve 100 percent integration; and
4. the form the vertical relationship takes. This does not necessarily mean ownership and full control of the integrated activities. Instead it could take any one of a number of different forms of joint venture.

If vertical integration is to be put to good use, the key in each case is to define these four characteristics, as no optimum breadth, level, or form of vertical integration applies to all companies and all circumstances.

Consequently, when deciding whether to integrate vertically, a very careful analysis must be made of the possible implications. The meaning and magnitude of these repercussions will vary, depending on the conditions of the industry in which the business is operating (i.e., volatility, the stage in the life cycle, uncertainty in the growth of sales, the industry's state of development, and the characteristics of rival companies), the bargaining power the company has over suppliers and clients, the company's aspirations and objectives, and its capacity to achieve them.

As discussed, vertical integration can offer big advantages, but it can also be a source of equally big problems and risks. As Harrigan (1983) warns, vertical integration is a double-edged sword and must be used very skillfully if a company's situation is to improve.

The vertical integration strategy has been used relatively seldom by the world's Top 10 hotel chains with the greatest number of rooms. Most of these chains, which are almost all North American, have opted for horizontal integration. However, so far the leaders of the European hotel industry, specifically the Spanish hotel chains, have not regarded horizontal concentrations as a way of strengthening their position in relation to the big tour operators. Instead they have chosen to integrate directly, as some of the following examples show.

EXAMPLES

Preussag

In the space of just two years[3] the Preussag consortium's tourism division, TUI (previously known as Hapag Touristik Union), has become the world's biggest vacation producer.

In 1841 Thomas Cook organized a train journey from Leicester to Loughborough for one shilling per person. One and a half centuries later his company helped form part of one of the biggest tourism groups in the world: the Preussag consortium.

The Preussag industrial group entered the tourism business relatively recently, when it purchased Hapag-Lloyd in 1997. A year later, with Hapag Touristik Union (HTU), it became Europe's leading tourism group. The result is that increasing numbers of tourists organize

their vacations through Preussag. For example, they make a reservation at one of the First, Hapag-Lloyd, or L'tur travel agencies; they fly
in airlines belonging to Hapag-Lloyd; and they stay in hotels owned
by the tour operator TUI, such as the Robinson Club.[4]

The chairman of the company would like to transform Preussag
into a vertically integrated tourism consortium, which would be active in all areas of the package vacation business, and he aims to increase its gross profits from the current figure of 3.6 to 5 percent. To
do this, he wants to increase Preussag's ownership of hotels in
vacation destinations, and in the next four years Preussag will buy
40,000 beds in order to double the number of clients stay in the consortium's own hotels.[5]

Given this process of concentration, German analysts say that if,
until now, tourists have benefited from fierce competition among tour
operators, the future is one big question mark. What will happen
when there are no independent hotels, travel agencies, charter flights,
and tour operators?

Airtours

In 2000, the British tour operator Airtours[6] acquired 50 percent of
the share capital of the Hotetur hotel chain. The other 50 percent was
retained by Teinver, the holding company that owns Hotetur. Teinver
also received 1.15 percent of Airtours' share capital, with a stock
market value of approximately 23.6 million euros. In addition, Airtours paid 23.6 million euros in cash, giving Hotetur[7] sufficient liquidity to carry out a number of projects that it had in the pipeline.

This transaction was yet another move in the tour operator's strategy of Spanish expansion. The chairman considers the deal an interesting step forward in Airtours' expansion into the hotel sector in key
destinations. Airtours' growth plans include control over a greater
number of hotel beds.

In March 2000, Airtours owners also purchased the entire share
capital of the Hoteles Globales hotel chain. The cost of the operation
amounted to 72 million euros, paid in cash. Under the terms of the
agreement between both parties, Hoteles Globales transferred the
ownership and operational control of its Hotel Don Pedro to Airtours.
Hoteles Globales retained the ownership of its other twenty-seven

hotels in Majorca, Minorca, Ibiza, Tenerife, Fuerteventura, and the Costa del Sol, but transferred the operational control to Airtours under a fifteen-year contract with purchase rights.

Carlson Hospitality Worldwide

Carlson Hospitality Worldwide is the joint owner (with Accor) of the travel agency Carlson Wagonlit Travel. The Carlson Wagonlit network has over 5,000 travel agencies in more than 140 countries, and it employs 11,800 workers who serve over 50,000 clients, generating an annual turnover of 11.5 billion dollars. As is logical, its clients tend to be directed toward hotels belonging to the travel agency's two owners, Carlson Hospitality Worldwide and Accor, giving the companies a big advantage over their competitors.

Carlson Hospitality Worldwide is also the sole owner of the travel wholesaler Inspirations. In addition, Carlson has shares in Caledonian Airways, a United Kingdom charter airline company. Its cruise line business is managed by the Carlson Cruises Worldwide division,[8] under the supervision of Carlson Hospitality. Thanks to this relationship, Carlson Cruises Worldwide benefits from technological support and a state-of-the-art bookings department. The company's employees offer a very high-quality service. Ninety-eight percent of its clients say their expectations were surpassed, and 95 percent say they would travel again with this cruise line.[9]

Accor

Accor, with its headquarters in Paris, is listed on the French capital's stock exchange. It has extensive interests in the travel and leisure business, headed by Carlson Wagonlit Travel as already mentioned. This is a 50/50 joint venture with the North American Carlson Companies (initiated in 1994 and completed in 1997). The latter is one of the world's five leading travel agencies. This alliance could have repercussions for their hotel-related business activities. As already mentioned, Carlson Wagonlit's business partner is the Carlson Group, based in the United States, whose brand names compete directly with some of Accor's brand names. Carlson and Accor both using Carlson Wagonlit to boost their hotel turnovers could lead to a conflict of interests. If, for example, Accor wished to double the number of bookings that its travel agencies receive, would Carlson insist on doing the same?

Accor also owns two tour operators (Accor Tour and Frantour), two catering companies (Lenôtre and Gemeaz Cusin), and, since 1998, Accor is the sole owner of Atria (a conference center management company). In 1999, Accor sold 50 percent of its Europcar shares to the Volkswagen car manufacturer.

First Choice and Barceló Empresas

The executives of the British tour operator First Choice and Barceló Empresas signed a strategic agreement[10] in April 2000, leading to a merger between the international tour operator and the Viajes Barceló division. As a result of the alliance, Barceló acquired control of a large part of the new integrated group's share capital, while also becoming the listed company's reference shareholder in a transaction totaling 222.4 million euros.

This move by First Choice can be interpreted as yet another step in its progressive rise up the ladder of the top European tour operators. With its recent acquisition of tour operators belonging to the Ten Tours group,[11] First Choice has held fifth place in the list that the German magazine *FVW* compiles each year.

At the same time, Barceló Empresas and First Choice have retained an option to form a joint venture for the Spanish hotel business. Barceló would provide fifteen of its fully owned Spanish hotels and First Choice would need to supply at least 300 million euros so as to have a 50 percent shareholding in the resulting hotel company. This money would be used to acquire new hotels in Spain, and Barceló Hotels & Resorts would retain the management of all of them.

Cendant Corporation

In 1999, Cendant Corporation sold its car rental division, by means of a series of leasing contracts including a purchase option, to AVIS for about 5.1 billion dollars. With part of the funds obtained from the sale of the car rental division, Cendant Corporation leaders managed to deal with the extraordinary losses that the company had suffered in

1997 following a merger between CUC International and HFS Incorporated. Cendant leaders have recovered their profit-making rhythm and have begun a process of expansion, commencing with the repurchase of AVIS for 930 million dollars. The purchase agreement also included PHH Arval, the world's second biggest car management company, and Wright Express, a leading nationwide supplier of fuel and vehicle maintenance smart cards.

In October 2001, Cendant Corporation acquired Galileo.[12] The deal represents a big change in direction for the megatourism group with its entry into the Global Distribution System (GDS) industry, a sector that is traditionally controlled by airline companies. The deal cost 1.8 billion dollars, and the strategic takeover of Galileo will enable Cendant Corporation to unite all its companies under the umbrella of one online platform. According to company managers, Cendant's strategy is to unite its online potential with its offline infrastructure.

Sol Meliá and Iberia

Sol Meliá and Iberia Airlines have entered into a joint venture that is a landmark in the history of the Spanish tourist industry, as it integrated companies that are leaders in each of their respective business segments.

The strategy led to the creation of Viva Tours, a tour operator that has produced big synergies between the companies. Viva Tours enables them to deal with a market that is increasingly competitive and mature, to the mutual benefit of all the companies involved.[13] After the first phase in Spain, the company leaders will center all of their efforts on the competitive European market to find a gap in the business of attracting tourists to Spain.

Coinciding with the entry into the Spanish market of America Online (AOL), via its Prodigios Internet portal, Sol Meliá (the founder of this ambitious e-business project) has created an independent travel agency under the name meliaviajes.com, which will be solely responsible for all the leisure and travel products marketed by this portal. Sol Meliá's involvement in the "AOL Avant" portal, as its sole supplier of leisure and travel products, guarantees the new agency access to 1 million Spanish users. The anticipated investment capital for the development of meliaviajes.com is 18 million euros.

According to the vice chairman of Sol Meliá, Sebastián Escarrer, meliaviajes.com was created to become the leading virtual travel agency in the Spanish- and Portuguese-speaking world.

In 2003, an agreement was reached between the executives of Sol Meliá and the British portal Lastminute.com.[14] The main consequence was meliaviajes.com's incorporation of the Spanish version of Lastminute.com. Sol Meliá became the owner of 70 percent of the Spanish Lastminute Web site, while the British company still controlled 30 percent of its Spanish portal, in a significant business operation that highlights the change that the online travel agency sector has undergone. These operations must be associated with other similar ones that have taken place on an international level, including deals as significant as USA Networks' acquisition of Expedia.

Sol Meliá leaders have indicated that the main purpose of this initiative is to take advantage of the synergies that can be produced between both multichannel agents, as well as to improve the promotion and sales of the group's hotels by using the Internet. The operation was also regarded as a way of cutting costs for both companies while facilitating the joint development of commercial activities.

Grupo Marsans

The main shareholders of Grupo Marsans, Gonzalo Pascual and Gerardo Díaz, also own most of the share capital of Air Plus, Viajes Marsans (a retail travel agency), Hotetur (a hotel chain), Viajes Internacional Express (a business travel specialist), Trapsa (a road transport company), and Pullmantur and Trapsatur (tour operators). They also control Spanair and its subsidiaries Club de Vacaciones and AeBal. They also own 38.5 percent of Tiempo Libre-Mundicolor and 25 percent of Mundosocial.

Grupo Iberostar

Grupo Iberostar operates in the hotel industry (Iberostar Hotels & Resorts), in the retail travel business (Viajes Iberia), in the travel wholesale business (Iberojet), in the reception trade (Iberoservice), the charter flight business (Iberworld), and the air services industry

(Aerobalear). It also holds shares in Mundosocial, Viva Tours, and Tiempo Libre.

Grupo Globalia

Grupo Globalia is composed of the following companies: Air Europa, Viajes Halcón, Travelplan, and Globalia Hotels & Resorts Inmobiliarios.

Nikko

In the transport sector, Nikko, a subsidiary of Japan Airlines (JAL), has carried out hotel deals all along JAL's network of airline routes, while Suissôtel has done the same with its partner Swissair.

SUMMARY

A fully vertically integrated company is one whose activities cover the entire production chain for a certain type of good, from the obtainment of raw materials to the delivery of the finished product to the consumer. In this chapter we analyzed the reasons why company leaders might choose this growth strategy instead of another. We saw how, historically, the benefits of vertical integration far outweighed the drawbacks, although now, given the sheer size of today's big corporations, there are fewer advantages due to their loss of flexibility and the huge organizational problems this causes. Consequently, the owners of the world's biggest hotel chains have generally chosen not to diversify. In some cases, they have even chosen the opposite strategy: vertical disintegration. In contrast, European holiday hotel owners have opted for vertical integration due to the importance of the tour operator, as demonstrated by the cases analyzed in this chapter. One remarkable example of vertical integration is Preussag, which has become the world's biggest holiday company through its tourist division (TUI Group).

Chapter 5

Horizontal Integration

THE THEORY

Horizontal integration takes place when several companies, all involved in the same level of the production chain, join forces to achieve a greater degree of concentration in a particular industry. Company owners integrate in this way to increase their purchasing power in relation to their suppliers and to increase their control of the distribution and sales of their product in the marketplace (monopoly power). An extreme case of horizontal integration occurred in the mid-1970s, when the countries that produce and export cooking oil formed a cartel to raise the price of oil by multiplying its original price four times.

Authors who specialize in horizontal integration do not believe that all companies have one optimum size (although factories or exploitation activities, such as mines or farming operations, may). Nevertheless, they accept that certain effects can reduce average costs when either production or the scope of a company's business operations increases. In other words, they believe in economies of scale. When these effects raise the average costs, it is referred to as diseconomies of scale.

In this sense, discussions have been held on a series of positive or negative effects of factors on a company's size and growth. These factors have led to several different theories on how economies of scale are created. The now classic work by Robinson (1957) is an interesting basis for an examination of these effects. Robinson classifies these factors into technical, management-based, financial, sales-related, and risk-based factors.

Technical Factors

Technical factors partly determine a company's size. However, to what extent they determine its size and whether they operate in the same way and have the same interrelations as other factors do should be ascertained.

From a technical point of view, factories and exploitation activities may be better examples than companies, as a company can combine different technologies and financial processes involving differing degrees of diversification. Thus the factors that influence the size of a business premises or a factory are the division of labor, process integration, and process balancing.

One of the factors that can boost economies is the division of labor, as it contributes toward more efficient output. Remember that Adam Smith outlined several reasons for this, such as increased worker skills, time that is saved which would otherwise be lost when passing from one job to another, and the invention of numerous machines designed to make work easier.

If a worker always does the same task, he or she will necessarily achieve a high degree of specialization. This degree of specialization will increase if the worker is not forced to waste time moving from one task to another. One consequence is the long list of machines that have been invented to make processes less lengthy. However, to achieve this division of labor and degree of specialization, a company needs to be sufficiently large to benefit from their advantages, and this is impossible for a business with a very low output.

Another factor is process integration: the exact opposite of the division of labor system. In other words, several processes are grouped together instead of separated. Thus, instead of using several machines, for example, the same result is achieved with just one. The economies derived from this system are bigger, as this type of machine tends to be more costly.

Process balancing is based on the idea of harmonizing the capacity of different production factors, so that they are all used to their maximum capacity. This problem arises due to the indivisibility of some factors. The idea is to combine similar production factors of each type used in the production process so that optimum use is made of those factors with a variable capacity. Proportionally, the greater output there is, the fewer idle resources of each type there will be.

Management Factors

Over time, the concept of an *entrepreneur* has gradually changed. Originally this person supplied capital and managed a company, but now, in most cases, one group of people supply the capital and others manage the firm in exchange for remuneration.

Remember that one of the basic characteristics of entrepreneurs is the risk they run, depending on the validity of their forecasts. All the remaining functions are also attributable to a professional management executive.[1]

Leaders of large companies divide and decentralize management duties into many parts, thereby making optimum use of people's professional training and experience. Nevertheless, for everything to go smoothly, the whole organization must be coordinated. According to Robinson (1957), coordination means ensuring that decisions made by A do not conflict with actions taken by B, or vice versa.

Each time a new division of labor occurs or, in other words, each time a person's work is divided into two or more parts, the problem of how to coordinate this work arises. However, as a company grows, coordination becomes more complex because if initial errors are not rectified, they build up and can be put right only at a cost, which may be very high.

Many of today's authors conclude that no reason exists for there to be any practical limits to the economies of scale that can be obtained through an organization's growth and, therefore, that a company's expansion is not restricted by management factors. Undeniably mega-management systems involve higher costs, because the bigger a company is, the bigger its management budget will be, but whether average management costs must rise is not clear. Nevertheless, even if they were to rise, would the diseconomies exceed the economies? This rarely happens.

Financial Factors

In many sectors companies may begin with very little capital, expanding gradually as opportunities arise. Other businesses cannot be started unless a considerable amount of capital is supplied, which one person could not possibly provide. This is the case, for instance, of the railway industry or electricity companies. In other words, there is a minimum sectorial size.

When owners want to grow their companies, they can resort to internal or external systems of finance. In many countries, most of the capital invested in growth is taken from the company profits. This means that often, during the initial stages at least, expansion is limited by the company's performance. Small business owners have problems seeking financing, as not enough specialist institutions or specific channels provide mid- and long-term loans of a sufficient amount. This does not occur with large company owners, who have access to external finance, either through the money market or the investment market (on a short- or long-term basis, nationally and internationally). The advantage they have is the ease with which money can be obtained and the lower price they have to pay for a loan, as well as their ability to issue shares or debentures, which small company owners cannot do.

The Sales Factor

Does a market's size limit expansion? There are two possibilities. If demand for a product is limited and a company can produce only this one product, then the company's size is restricted by the demand. However, if the company can produce several different products, it can continue to develop by increasing or commencing the production of those products that do not have a limited demand. In this case, limited demand does not restrict the company's size.

Furthermore, in practice, if a demand has a limit, executives can take direct action through an active marketing policy and new product launches. Marketing and product diversification are both reasons why today's authors do not accept the theory that a company's size is limited by its market.

Large-scale purchases offer many advantages, such as the benefits of buying in bulk, with consequent reductions in prices by suppliers. In addition, a well-organized sales department has good buyers at its disposal who also help the company to economize. In contrast, the large-scale distribution of products has more drawbacks than benefits, because consumers logically expect this service to be included in the price of a product. It is therefore a source of diseconomies of scale. In addition to distribution costs, specific sales costs are incurred by a company's sales department, together with sales promotion costs. Bulk sales offer many advantages, as the fixed costs can be spread among the greatest possible number of units.

Market power and the opportunity to influence the decisions of the political and ruling classes, both of which are integral features of large companies, act as growth incentives. One of the factors that tends to lead to a company's growth is the entrepreneur's own interest in maximizing his or her business concern. As the development of the leaders of some of the economy's most dynamic sectors shows, company growth also facilitates access to systems of banking finance, a larger market, and product standardization.

Risk Factors

Because company leaders are unable to see into the future with any precision, they are forced to base their future plans on forecasts. However, these forecasts (calculated by anticipating the future results of specific types of action) are affected by certain likelihood coefficients. This is where the entrepreneur becomes uncertain of how reliable the forecasts are. Another possible risk can be caused by fluctuations in a variable that may be considered relatively easy to predict.

With a traditional method of analysis, entrepreneurs simply took the risk of a possible fluctuation for granted. They merely applied sufficient safety coefficients to cover their backs. In contrast, a modern method of analysis accepts that entrepreneurs can influence the demand in several ways, thus reducing both the uncertainty and the risk.

Another theory used by advocates of economies of scale to support their beliefs is Ansoff's (1965) concept of a synergy, proposed as part of his conception of a diversification-based growth strategy. As mentioned earlier, a synergy can be described as the effect produced by a combination of several different elements as compared with the separate effects of each individual element. A positive synergy would be considered to have occurred if the combined effect were greater than the sum of the individual effects.[2]

Hotel chains, in the broadest sense of the word (i.e., business organizations that run more than one hotel), are becoming more ubiquitous, and the experience of countries with the most developed tourist industries, such as the United States, indicates that hotel chains will become the dominant form of management in the future.

Running a chain is nothing new in the hotel trade. The management of several hotels by one organization has been common practice for over fifty years. Hotel chains really started to take off during the last years of World War II and immediately afterward. During this period the Hilton Hotels Corporation and Sheraton chains began to grow very rapidly in the United States. Executives of both speculated that the swiftest form of expansion would be to take over existing hotels. Both bought and sold properties so fast that a register of hotels was needed to keep up to date with their transactions. Both Hilton Hotels Corporation and Sheraton were said to be real estate agencies instead of hotel management companies.

Why did hotel chains undergo such considerable growth? The best reply, in a word, is efficiency. When faced with the strong competition of an efficiently run hotel chain, an independent hotel operator had three alternatives. First, he or she could try to compensate for the company's reduced business by lowering its maintenance costs and increasing room prices. This solution was popular but risky. Second, if the company had capital, the owner could take a chance and invest in alterations, modernization, and promotional activities. This method was adequate and has helped many hotels to remain independent. The third option was to sell the property, hoping to make some kind of profit before it was too late. This is why owners were able to expand their chains without building too many new hotels.

According to Ernest Henderson (personal communication), a former chairman of Sheraton Corporation of America, the main advantages of chains over independent hotels are as follows:

- *Purchases:* By making huge bulk purchases, from food to furniture, chains receive big discounts.
- *Staff:* A chain can afford to employ top specialists at all levels of hotel management (engineers, food control specialists, decorators, architects, accountants, sales experts, etc.) by simply sharing the costs among its numerous hotels. Few individual hotel operators can afford this type of specialization.
- *Promotion:* National publicity campaigns in newspapers and magazines are generally far too costly for independent hotels, but they can be very useful when the costs are split among forty-one hotels, for example. Each receives the maximum benefits of a nationwide campaign, while paying only a fraction of the costs.
- *Finance:* Big hotel groups have access to sources of finance that an individual hotel either does not have or may have but under much worse financial terms.

The competitive advantages that some countries, such as Spain, benefited from in the past led to a proliferation of independent hotels. However, the hotel industry is then highly fragmented and it is highly problematic when corrective measures are needed, such as those that the hotel business now faces (i.e., improving the quality of facilities, solving the problem of a shortage of basic infrastructure in some tourist resorts, improving workers' skills, incorporating computer technology into management processes, reducing individual hotels' execessive dependence on tour operators, etc.). All these problems share the characteristic that, in most cases, their solution is beyond the capacity of an independent entrepreneur. He or she then contemplates the possibility of joining forces with hotel owners who are in the same situation and are interested in improving their future prospects.

Until a few years ago, the Spanish market had still not been affected by merger- and acquisition-based horizontal integration strategies, but mention should be made of Sol Meliá's 2000 purchase of Tryp and the consolidation of this leading Spanish hotel group, which is also one of the world's top hotel businesses. However, among U.S. hotel chains this phenomenon is spectacularly dynamic and increasingly common.

The hotel demand is heavily concentrated on the European continent.[3] The process of horizontal concentration, which has enabled some leading tour operators to expand into other European markets, has intensified over the past few years with operations such as the purchase of Thomson by Preussag (which owns TUI) or the purchase of Thomas Cook by Neckermann, and Airtours' entry into the German market following the absorption of FTI. In Spain, only First Choice has made a grand entrance by buying the travel division of Grupo Barceló.

The next section is an exhaustive analysis of the size and growth rates of the world's ten biggest hotel chains: the maximum exponents of hotel companies' worldwide process of horizontal integration.

EXAMPLES

Table 5.1 shows the evolution of the hotel portfolios of the world's Top 10 hotel chains with the greatest number of rooms, while Table 5.2 shows the evolution of the Top 10 hotel chains' room portfolios.

The growth rates of each of the Top 10 hotel chains during the seven years from 1995 to January 2002 will be discussed next.

Cendant Corporation

Cendant Corporation is the world's largest hotel chain, with over 6,600 hotels and more than half a million rooms. The hotel chain increased its hotel portfolio by 56 percent and its room portfolio by 33 percent. In other words, it added almost thirty-three new hotels to its portfolio each month and sixty-three accommodation units per day (almost equivalent to three rooms per hour). Cendant Corporation's hotels have an average capacity of about eighty-four rooms.

Cendant Corporation underwent the greatest expansion in hotels and hotel rooms in 1999, with a growth rate of almost thirty-eight rooms per day (or three rooms every two hours), and a total increase in hotel rooms of 13,734. Its hotels increased at a rate of twenty-eight new properties per month, with a total increase of 337 hotels.

Cendant Corporation had the largest hotels in its portfolio in 1995, with an average capacity of ninety-eight rooms, while its smallest hotels correspond to January 2002, with almost eighty-four rooms per hotel.

TABLE 5.1. Hotel Portfolios of the World's Top 10 Hotels, 1995–January 2002

Hotels/Chain	1995	1998	1999	2000	January 2002
Cendant Corporation	4,243	5,978	6,315	6,455	6,624
Six Continents PLC*	2,523	2,738	2,886	3,096	3,274
Marriott International	977	1,686	1,880	2,099	2,398
Accor	2,378	2,666	3,234	3,488	3,654
Choice Hotels International	3,432	3,670	4,248	4,392	4,545
Hilton Hotels Corporation	223	250	1,700	1,895	1,986
Best Western International	3,462	3,814	4,037	4,065	4,052
Starwood Hotels & Resorts Worldwide	–	694	716	738	743
Carlson Hospitality Worldwide	313	548	616	716	788
Sol Meliá	203	246	260	338	350

Source: www.hostelmag.com.

*In the fourth quarter of 2002, the hotels and soft drink business of Six Continents PLC was listed as InterContinental Hotels Group PLC.

Six Continents Hotels

Together with Cendant Corporation, Six Continents Hotels was one of the only two hotel chains in the world with over half a million rooms. The company expanded by 751 hotels and 141,547 rooms. In other words, its hotel portfolio increased by 30 percent, with the inauguration of ten hotels per month, and its room portfolio increased by 38 percent, with almost sixty-five new accommodation units per day or three rooms per hour. The company's hotels had an average capacity of almost 160 rooms.

In 2001 Six Continents Hotels experienced a growth rate of fifty-seven rooms per day or 2.5 rooms per hour, and a total increase of 20,541 rooms. In 2000 its hotel portfolio underwent the greatest growth, with an increase of 17.5 hotels per month, or a total increase of 210 hotels.

It had the biggest hotels in its portfolio in 1998, with an average capacity of 169 rooms. This ratio gradually decreased to a 2002 figure of 156 rooms per hotel.

TABLE 5.2. The Top 10 Hotel Chains' Room Portfolios, 1995–January 2002

Rooms/Chain	1995	1998	1999	2000	January 2002
Cendant Corporation	415,756	528,896	542,630	541,313	553,771
Six Continents PLC	369,525	461,434	471,680	490,531	511,072
Marriott International	203,593	328,300	355,900	390,469	435,983
Accor	268,256	291,770	354,652	389,437	415,774
Choice Hotels International	296,723	305,171	338,254	350,351	362,549
Hilton Hotels Corporation	93,717	85,000	290,000	317,823	327,487
Best Western International	282,062	301,899	313,247	307,737	306,851
Starwood Hotels & Resorts Worldwide	–	225,014	217,651	227,042	224,467
Carlson Hospitality Worldwide	80,860	106,244	114,161	129,234	135,066
Sol Meliá	47,938	65,586	69,178	82,656	85,987

Source: www.hostelmag.com.

Marriott International

Marriott International's hotel portfolio increased by 1,421 hotels and its room portfolio by 232,390 rooms. In other words, its hotel portfolio grew by 145 percent, with the inauguration of almost twenty new hotels per month. Meanwhile, its room portfolio increased by 114 percent, with 106 new accommodation units per day, which is equivalent to almost four rooms per hour. The company's hotels have an average capacity of 182 rooms.

Marriott underwent the greatest expansion in hotels and rooms in 2001, with a growth rate of almost 125 rooms per day or over five rooms per hour. This led to a total increase of 45,514 rooms. Regarding new additions to its hotel portfolio, it expanded at a rate of only twenty-five per month, with a total increase of 299 hotels.

Marriott International had the largest capacity hotels in its portfolio in 1995, with 208 rooms per hotel. This ratio steadily decreased to a 2002 figure of 182 rooms per hotel.

Nevertheless, as a result of the events of September 11, 2001, Marriott International and the other hotel chains analyzed in this book delayed their expansion plans. John Marriott III, the executive vice chairman of Marriott International, confirmed that recessions are also moments that can create big opportunities—the chance to re-focus the company's progress or acquire properties—because in these more difficult times it is important to maintain clients and win over new ones (www.editur.com). By a twist of fate, this declaration was made by Marriott just two hours before the Twin Towers collapsed on one of the company's properties.

Accor

Accor increased its hotel portfolio with the incorporation of 1,276 new hotels, while its room portfolio grew by 147,518. This means that both its hotel and room portfolios increased 54 percent, with the inauguration of almost eighteen hotels per month and sixty-seven accommodation units per day (or 2.8 rooms per hour). The company's hotels have an average capacity of 114 rooms.

Accor experienced the strongest growth, in terms of hotels and rooms, in 1999, with a growth rate of 172 rooms per day or over seven rooms per hour. This led to a total increase of almost 63,000 rooms. Meanwhile, it incorporated forty-seven new hotels per month, with a total increase of 568 hotel properties.

Accor's 2002 portfolio includes the largest-capacity hotels so far, with 114 rooms per hotel. This ratio remained practically the same for the past six years.[4]

Choice Hotels International

Choice Hotels International is the second largest hotel chain in the world in terms of the number of hotels it owns, with over 4,500 hotels. This American chain expanded by incorporating 1,113 new hotels and 65,826 rooms. This means that its hotel portfolio rose by 32 percent, with over fifteen new hotels per month, and its room portfolio by 22 percent, with thirty new accommodation units per day (equal to almost 1.25 rooms per hour). The company's hotels have an average capacity of eighty rooms.

Its strongest growth year, from the perspective of hotels and rooms, was 1999, with a growth rate of almost ninety-one rooms per day (equivalent to almost four rooms per hour), and a total increase of almost 33,083 rooms. As for hotels, it acquired forty-eight new ones each month, leading to a total increase of 578 new hotels.

It had the largest hotels in its portfolio in January 1995, with an average capacity of eighty-six rooms, whereas its smallest hotels correspond to January 2002, with almost eighty rooms per hotel.

Hilton Hotels Corporation

Hilton Hotels Corporation added 1,763 hotels and over 233,000 rooms to its portfolios. This means that its total number of hotels multiplied ninefold, with twenty-four new hotels per month. Its total number of rooms multiplied by 3.5, with 107 new accommodation units per day (equivalent to almost 4.5 rooms per hour). The company's hotels have an average capacity of 165 rooms per hotel.

It underwent the greatest growth in hotels and rooms in 1999, with a growth rate of 562 rooms per day, or over twenty-three rooms per hour. This represented a total increase of 205,000 rooms. As for hotels, it acquired 121 new properties per month, leading to a total increase of 1,450.

Hilton Hotels Corporation owned its largest average capacity hotels in 1995, with 420 rooms per hotel. This ratio decreased over the years to a 2002 average of 165 rooms per hotel.

Best Western International

Best Western International increased its hotel portfolio by 590 hotels and its room portfolio by almost 25,000 rooms, meaning that its hotel portfolio increased by 17 percent, with eight new hotels each month, and its room portfolio by 9 percent, with eleven new accommodation units per day. The company's hotels average seventy-six rooms per hotel.

The company underwent the strongest growth in hotels in 1999, with a growth rate of thirty-one rooms per day, equivalent to just over one room per hour. This led to a total increase of 11,348 rooms. It increased its hotel properties at a rate of 18.5 hotels per month, with a total growth of 223 hotels.

Best Western International had its largest average capacity hotels in 1995, with a mean ratio of eighty-one rooms per hotel. This ratio hardly changed, oscillating between eighty-three rooms in 1994 and seventy-six in 2002.

Starwood Hotels & Resorts Worldwide

Starwood Hotels & Resorts Worldwide heads the world's Top 10 hotel chains with the greatest capacity properties. Although the American chain acquired forty-nine new hotels between 1998 and 2002, it reduced its rooms by 547. The company's hotels have an average capacity of 302 rooms.

In 2000 the company underwent the highest growth, with a daily growth rate of almost twenty-six new rooms (or one room per hour), and a total of 9,391 rooms. It acquired almost two new hotels per month, leading to a total of twenty-two.

In 1998 Starwood Hotels & Resorts Worldwide had its largest capacity hotels, with 324 rooms per hotel. This ratio has gone down over the years to a 2002 figure of 302 rooms per hotel.

Carlson Hospitality Worldwide

Carlson Hospitality Worldwide is the largest unlisted hotel company in the world. The company expanded by incorporating 475 new hotels and 54,206 rooms. In other words, its hotel portfolio grew by 151 percent, with over six new hotels per month, and its room portfolio by 67 percent, with almost twenty-five new accommodation units per day, or one room per hour. The company's hotels have an average capacity of almost 171 rooms.

In 2000 the company experienced the strongest growth in hotels and rooms, with a growth rate of forty-one rooms per day or almost two rooms per hour, representing a total increase of 15,073 rooms. In terms of hotels, the company acquired eight new hotels per month, with a total increase of 100 new properties.

Carlson Hospitality Worldwide had the largest average capacity hotels in its portfolio in 1995, with 258 rooms per hotel. This ratio has gradually decreased to a 2002 figure of 171 rooms per hotel.

Sol Meliá

Sol Meliá expanded by incorporating 147 new hotels and 38,049 rooms. This means that its hotel portfolio rose by 72 percent, with the inauguration of two hotels each month. The company's room portfolio increased by 79 percent, with seventeen new accommodation units per day or three rooms every four hours.

In 2000 Sol Meliá underwent the greatest growth in hotels and rooms, with a growth rate of thirty-seven new rooms each day, or three rooms every two hours, leading to a total increase of almost 13,500 new rooms. It acquired 6.5 new hotels per month, with a total increase of seventy-eight new properties.

Sol Meliá had the largest average capacity hotels in its portfolio in 1998, with 267 rooms per hotel. By January 2002, this figure had fallen to an average of 146 rooms per hotel.

Analysis

The hotel industry's degree of concentration is increasing. As an illustration, the Top 5's joint portfolio in the time period analyzed was bigger than the Top 200's joint portfolio was in the early 1980s. In addition, practically *half* the Top 10's joint portfolio was owned by three chains alone: Cendant Corporation, Six Continents Hotels, and Choice Hotels International.

The Top 10[5] accounted for 20 percent of the world's total hotels. Their room portfolio was higher than that of the remaining 190 chains that made up the Top 200, which in turn represented 35 percent of the world's total hotels. The increase in the Top 10's portfolio accounts for 50 percent of the world hotel trade's increase in hotel rooms.

During the period of our analysis, the Top 10 grew at a rate of 138 new hotels per month and 491 rooms per day. This growth rate, over a period of less than six months, is equivalent to Sol Meliá's entire portfolio. During this period, all the Top 10 chains increased their hotel and room portfolios, with the exception of Starwood Hotels & Resorts Worldwide, which reduced its portfolio of rooms by just 547.

The hotel chains that underwent the greatest international expansion during the period of our analysis were Hilton Hotels Corporation and Marriott International, with a growth rate of 106 rooms per day. In third place is Accor, with a difference of forty rooms per day. In terms of hotels, Cendant Corporation experienced the greatest worldwide growth with thirty-three new hotels per month, followed by Hilton Hotels Corporation with twenty-four hotels per month.

U.S. chains played a predominant role in the world's Top 10 hotel chains. All the Top 10 hotel chains were based in the states, except for Accor (which is French), Sol Meliá (based in Spain), and Six Continents Hotels (which had head offices in England, although the head office of the holding's hotel division was in the United States). For the past twenty years Holiday Inn, HFS, and Cendant Corporation have headed the world's Top 10 chains with the greatest number of hotel rooms. All of them are North American.

Japanese hotel chains have never achieved the growth rates or international success of Japanese companies from other business sectors, such as the automobile or electronics industries. The paralysis or even decline suffered by Japanese chains is evident in the evolution of the portfolios of the country's leading chains, such as Nikko Hotels, Ana Hotels, and Okura, without forgetting the sales figures of the InterContinental and Westin brand names, which belonged to Seibu Saison and Aoki, respectively.

In the late 1990s, the owners of big international hotel corporations began an unprecedented race to achieve the greatest degree of horizontal concentration. In late 1995, the Granada Group fired the starting pistol. On November 22, while he was out hunting (a hobby that had serious negative repercussions on his image), Sir Rocco Forte learned that the Granada Group had made a takeover bid for the control of Forte Hotels, a company controlled by the family, even though they only owned 9 percent of the share capital. Sir Rocco failed in his attempt to convince the company's shareholders (many of whom had more shares than the Forte family) of the need to turn down the takeover bid. Granada invested the equivalent of almost 3 billion euros in the operation.

Nevertheless, the best-publicized operation of the decade began on January 13, 1997, when Hilton Hotels Corporation, which was in the midst of merging its marketing, sales, and booking networks with Hilton International, announced a takeover bid for ITT Corporation for the astounding sum of 10.5 billion dollars. ITT's resistance attracted the attention of a third group, Starwood Hotels & Resorts Worldwide, which had already closed a deal for the purchase of Westin for almost 1.6 billion dollars. Starwood finally pulled the deal off. The business transaction concluded thirteen months later, at a cost of 14.6 billion dollars.

The owners of Starwood Hotels & Resorts Worldwide applied for loans equivalent to 5.4 billion euros, and they were forced to sell assets such as their casino division (Caesars), which was purchased by Park Place for over 2.7 billion euros. From having control over one hundred hotels in the United States, they suddenly multiplied their assets almost sevenfold, acquiring brand names as prestigious as Westin, Sheraton, or The Luxury Collection, but they did not stop there.[6]

Fights to take over hotel groups have occurred on other occasions. In 1997, after buying the North American chain Red Lion, Doubletree executives (with 236 hotels and over 55,000 rooms) signed an 890 million dollar takeover agreement for Renaissance (with 146 hotels under management or franchise contracts and over 45,000 rooms). However, Marriott International leaders appeared on the scene and pushed up the bid to 1 billion. Without even hesitating, Renaissance leaders broke their word with Doubletree. The latter promptly reacted by reaching an agreement for Promus (with 1,136 hotels and 172,000 rooms) to take over its properties. In turn, Promus was purchased by Hilton Hotels Corporation in late 1999 for 4 billion dollars, meaning that Hilton Hotels Corporation bought Promus, which had acquired Doubletree, which had bought Red Lion. Three business deals allowed Hilton Hotels Corporation to increase its portfolio from 226 in 1995 to 1,986 in January 2002, with 327,687 rooms and 85,000 employees.

In February 1998, Six Continents, the owner of Holiday Hospitality, was the leading protagonist of another prime example of concentration when it purchased the assets of InterContinental for 2.9 billion dollars in cash. The operation was a huge success, adding 187 hotels and 65,000 rooms to the 2,400 hotels it already controlled, while also giving it access to a type of clientele in which it had not previously specialized. Although Six Continents was perfectly positioned in the mid-range segment, thanks to its different Holiday Inn brand names, its luxury division (Crowne Plaza) barely had an international presence. In contrast, the company it took over, InterContinental, was in just the opposite position: it dominated the luxury hotel market, but its mid-range brand name (Forum) was scarcely known.

Six Continents' eagerness to expand continued. In 2000 the owners bought 90 percent of Bristol (with 112 hotels in the United States and Canada), a company in which they already had a 10 percent stake. They also acquired Southern Pacific Hotels Corporation, with fifty-nine hotels in the Asian-Pacific area. In France, one of the companies that has most obviously made a bid for increased concentration is the Accor Group. In June 1999, together with the Colony and Blackstone investment fund companies, which own the Savoy Group, Accor acquired the hotel assets of the French company Vivendi.[7]

Two months later, Accor caused a stir in the United States by adding the 322 hotels and 37,000 rooms of the Red Roof chain to its Motel 6 brand name. After completing the 1.1 billion dollar operation, Accor executives set in motion a leaseback program (the sale of a property, after which the buyer then leases it back to the seller) for 288 of its Motel 6 properties, thus ensuring their management control for a period of twenty years including renewal rights. In France, too, the second and third biggest hotel groups merged. Envergure (with 630 hotels and majority ownership of the Campanile and Première Classe brand names) bought Hôtels & Compagnie in June 1999 (with 297 hotels, and Climat de France as its best known division). The end result was a total of almost 1,000 hotels in the economically priced end of the market, in other words a substantial part of the French market.

This tendency to integrate has also affected business consortiums. Leaders of Best Western International and Consort decided to merge their United Kingdom assets in 2000, creating the biggest hotel consortium in the country under the Best Western brand name, with almost 400 hotels commercialized from Consort's former head offices. All of these examples are significant of the trend toward globalization detected in the top echelons of the international hotel trade during the past five years.[8]

SUMMARY

Horizontal integration occurs when several companies, all involved in the same level of the production chain, join forces to achieve a greater degree of concentration in a particular industry. In this chapter, a careful analysis was made of factors that influence the degree of horizontal integration and the growth of this phenomenon, particularly in the hotel trade where, for over fifty years now, single organizations commonly run several hotels. As a result, this chapter analyzed the horizontal integration process of some of the world's leading hotel companies, using the Top 10 with the largest room portfolios as representative examples. Two particularly significant exponents were the hotel chains Cendant Corporation and Six Continents PLC, each with over half a million rooms.

Chapter 6

Diagonal Integration

THE THEORY

The main feature of diagonal integration is not the fact that companies involved in the same stage of production join together to influence the industry's concentration levels (as occurs in horizontal integration), that they try to control several stages of production (as occurs in vertical integration), or that they engage in other activities in order to minimize risks (as in diversification). Instead, the main characteristic is that companies with related activities join forces to cut costs and have a more direct relationship with consumers.

In the tourist industry, diagonal integration means forming links with companies that belong to sectors other than the tourist industry. Some authors refer to it as conglomerate diversification (Martín Rojo, 1988).

The key elements of diagonal integration are based on the concept of forging a closer relationship with consumers so as to reduce costs by *economies of scope, systems gains,* and *synergies.* In contrast, vertical integration is supply oriented, whereas diversification is investment oriented.

Information technologies provide the means for companies to achieve diagonal integration. These companies can use them both to identify their target consumers and to integrate the production of the services they offer.

Diagonal integration has two major implications. First, company employees will not know how to define the limits of their work and responsibilities. Second, diagonal integration will widen the company's field of competition, because the company's rivals will no longer come only from the sector in which the company competes.

As already mentioned, diagonal integration offers certain major advantages. Diagonal integration provides the opportunity to benefit from *economies of scope,* which means that lower costs can be achieved by the joint production of a series of goods. These economies differ from economies of scale in that economies of scope depend on the variety of goods produced, whereas economies of scale depend on the volume of goods produced. Economies of scope are not designed to replace economies of scale, but to reinforce them, as companies that use both types will be more effective in the midterm than companies that use only scale economies.

Economies of scope exist in the production of product 1 and 2, if

$$C(q^1, q^2) < C(q^1, 0) + C(0, q^2),$$
$$\text{for } q^1 > 0 \text{ and } q^2 > 0,$$

where $C(q^1, q^2)$ is the company's minimum cost when producing q units of product 1 and q units of product 2, with an identical input price in both cases; $C(q^1, 0)$ is the company's minimum cost when producing q units of product 1 and zero units of product 2; and $C(0, q^2)$ is the company's minimum cost when producing q units of product 2 and zero units of product 1.

With economies of scope, a single company's joint production of two products is less costly than the joint costs of two companies each producing product 1 and product 2.

Diagonal integration also offers a series of benefits derived from the *synergies* of the management, operation, and organization of interrelated activities, where one activity can generate profits that serve to reinforce the rest. In turn, synergies can create economies of scope.

Diagonal integration offers *systems gains,* the benefits or economies that are produced due to the creation of links between different activities. Chains of activities are an example of these benefits, where each activity can share common databases. Systems gains can occur, for instance, when banks use the extensive information they hold on record about clients to offer them different services, such as travel opportunities or different types of insurance.

EXAMPLES

Companies such as American Express are diagonally integrated in order to offer consumer services (personal banking, credit cards, insurance, and travel services), in the hope that these consumers will use them at regular intervals throughout their lives. American Express Europe Ltd., for instance, generates one-third of its leisure sales through American Express credit cards.

Another example is United Airlines, which is capable of creating enormous synergies by linking its credit cards with its client-loyalty program. In this way, for each dollar users spend with their credit cards, they can obtain one free mile as part of United Airlines' frequent flier program.

The Barceló hotel chain carried out a joint venture in August 1998 with two companies, FCC (Fomento de Construcciones y Contratas) and Argentaria, aimed at revolutionizing the Spanish hotel industry. The original idea was to create a new hotel company, Grubarges, which would embrace all the industry's production process. This was achieved because the activities of the three companies participating in the project fully complemented the hotel trade.[1]

In turn, the three partners then created two divisions within Grubarges: Grubarges Inversión, responsible for channeling investments and for the ownership of the hotels, and Grubarges Gestión, in charge of the hotels' management.

As part of the project, eleven hotels were acquired by Grubarges Inversión: nine that had previously been owned by Argentaria and two by Barceló. The objective was to create a hotel chain within a period of one and a half years with over forty hotels in Europe and America. The capital that was invested amounted to approximately 600 million euros. The project, which did not rule out the inclusion of new partners (all from the hotel industry), also contemplated the long-term possibility of listing Grubarges Inversión on the stock exchange in order to finance the company's international expansion.

All the companies benefited from the joint venture: FCC achieved an old aspiration, to enter the tourist industry; the Barceló Group formed a partnership with two important suppliers of financial support, so as to accelerate the growth of its hotel division; and Argentaria managed to "relocate" part of its real estate assets acquired during the crisis of the 1990s.

Owners of the Spanish hotel chain NH made a takeover bid for the entire share capital of the Sotogrande property company, amounting to 86.5 million euros. The Spanish hotel chain formed an alliance with the American property group Equity International to develop projects in Latin America equivalent to 100 million dollars. Leaders chose the Italian company Jolly as their European partner by acquiring a minority yet significant share of its capital (19 percent).

In addition to the support of the investment company Mercapital, Occidental Hoteles chose the Caixa Savings Bank as its partner (or perhaps it was the other way around). The financial entity controls 27.5 percent of the hotel chain's share capital and it has managed Occidental Hoteles, which will invest 601 million euros in its short-term expansion, as of 1999.

SUMMARY

Diagonal integration can mainly be said to occur when companies with related activities join forces in order to cut costs and forge closer links with consumers. The cornerstones of this strategy are therefore economies of scope, systems gains, and synergies. Although hotel chains have not shown any mass tendency to use this strategy, the chapter closed by looking at key examples of diagonal integration in the international tourist industry. One outstanding example is Grubarges, a hotel company that covers the hotel industry's entire production process from finance and construction to hotel management, created as a result of a joint venture involving a hotel chain (Barceló Hotels & Resorts), a bank (Argentaria), and a building developer (Fomento de Construcciones y Contratas).

Chapter 7

Acquisitions and Mergers

THE THEORY

Before examining the problems involved in acquisitions and mergers is a good time to explain the difference between *internal growth* and *external growth.*

Internal growth is based on investment within the company itself, whereas *external growth* is the result of acquiring, buying shares in, controlling, or cooperating with other companies.

External growth is clearly the method that company executives most widely prefer, including those of hotel chains, observed in the strong trend in developed capitalist countries toward industrial, financial, and tourism-related concentrations during the past few decades. Several reasons account for this phenomenon.

Normally, the owners of one company purchase another company or merge with it for the following reasons: to reduce competition; to increase the company's efficiency and profitability (particularly if a synergy exists between both companies); to improve the stability of results; to find an outlet for surplus funds and/or an outlet for investment when a good opportunity arises; for fiscal reasons, etc. In turn, executives allow their companies to be taken over or give others access to shares in order to increase their growth capacity through the injection of new resources, to increase their efficiency, to raise the value of shares, to solve management problems, etc. (Glueck, 1980).

In addition to these reasons, we can also outline a number of other advantages that external growth offers companies in comparison with internal growth: (1) It allows a company to perform faster than it would if further internal investment was made. This gain in time is particularly important in an unstable environment. (2) It enables a company to increase its market share without the risk of possible overcapacity. This, for example, is particularly important in mature sectors. (3) Sometimes it is the only way of acquiring technical and human resources or intangible assets for which no market exists. Likewise, it can also be the only way to penetrate a specific market. This is the case, for instance, of internationalization in a country with certain legal restrictions, such as Brazil or India.

However, external growth is not without difficulties or drawbacks, and these may sometimes lead to worse results than the anticipated ones or even to negative results.

For example, a fundamental, commonly mentioned problem is how to carry out an assessment of the company to be acquired or the companies involved in the merger. This is always tricky, despite developments in the field of financial analysis. However, human problems can be more dangerous. Structural or cultural conflicts can give rise to a negative synergy, thus reducing the company's performance, or even leading to the operation's failure. Therefore, an external growth decision must be seen as part of a clearly defined growth strategy. This involves a mandatory, careful analysis of candidate companies' compatibility with the firm's structure, strategy, and business culture, followed by attention to business mechanisms after the acquisition or merger.

However, empirical studies show that company leaders often fail to attempt an internal or external growth strategy simply because it is not a viable possibility (due to a lack of external growth potential, for instance), or because this type of strategy is not considered a decision as such since the leaders are more liable to act on impulse, offering a strategic response at a given moment in time if they have the ability to do so, despite the disadvantages that this entails.

Nevertheless, these two types of growth often complement each other rather than being opposites, and they form part of a global growth strategy (Morvan, 1985).

One of the external growth strategies with the greatest repercussions in the past century was the strategy of mergers and acquisitions. Given the sheer number and importance of the companies involved, together with the economic and political repercussions, a great deal of literature has been published on the subject, aimed at accounting for its significance or explaining the causes of this phenomenon.

When studying this type of strategy, the first step is to define what exactly a merger, acquisition, or even absorption means.

Leaving aside the legal aspects, a *merger* occurs when two or more companies that are generally of a similar size agree to join forces. This then leads to the creation of a new company, into which all their former resources (or assets) are invested. The original companies are then dissolved.

In contrast, an *acquisition* is when one company purchases another or acquires shares in it, via a number of different procedures, so that the first company acquires control or full ownership of the second. With an acquisition, the takeover company and the company that is taken over might retain the same legal status.

Finally, an *absorption* occurs when one company acquires another and, generally speaking, the second company disappears.

From the perspective of a strategic analysis, nothing differentiates these three options. Consequently, they are normally studied in conjunction, and the words merger and acquisition are used indistinctly. We will follow the same method, except in cases where there might be important implications.

Several different reasons are given to explain why these strategies are used. These can be analyzed by means of a number of explanatory theories, each based on a series of objectives that can be achieved by using these strategies. The seven theories (Trautwein, 1990) we will explore are the efficiency theory; the monopoly theory; the raider theory; the valuation theory; the empire-building theory; the process theory; and the disturbance theory, all of which are shown in Figure 7.1, together with the reasons behind them.

1. According to the *efficiency theory,* acquisitions and mergers are carried out to obtain financial, operational, and managerial synergies. *Financial synergies* are produced as a result of a decreased investment risk when unrelated cases of diversification are involved. An increase in size is another source of financial synergies, as it can facilitate access to capital at a lower cost, while also increasing companies' borrowing capacity. *Operational synergies* are obtained when marketing and/or production capacities and skills can be jointly used. *Management synergies* are produced thanks to the abilities and skills of managers joining the company as a result of the merger.

Mergers as a rational decision	The benefits of mergers for shareholders	Benefits from synergies	The efficiency theory
		Increased market power	The monopoly theory
		The increased wealth of takeover companies that take this initiative	The raider theory
		Net benefits through information	The valuation theory
	The benefits of mergers for managers or directors		The empire-building theory
	Mergers as the result of a process		The process theory
	Mergers as a macroeconomic phenomenon		The disturbance theory

FIGURE 7.1. Theories on Mergers or Acquisitions

However, if this type of strategy is justified by attributing it to a search for financial benefits, the results are rather unsatisfactory. Although financial reasons have been most commonly used as a justification, thereby generating the greatest number of theoretical and empirical studies, they may not be the main reason behind mergers or acquisitions. In fact, some evidence points to the fact that postmerger performance is worse than the merged companies' prior performance (Ravenscraft and Scherer, 1989; Caves, 1989). Other studies indicate that mergers' negative results are financially related.

2. *The monopoly theory.* According to this theory, mergers or acquisitions are carried out to improve companies' competitiveness. Horizontal mergers can reduce market competition. This phenomenon is what public authorities try to prevent by intervening in these kinds of mergers or acquisitions (e.g., via antitrust laws in the United States and, in general, via legislation to prevent restrictive business practices that limit competition). However, vertical mergers and those that lead to conglomerates can also create situations in which competition is restricted. In the first case, a client, for instance, can

have problems with supplies because the supplier has been taken over by a competitor. In the second case, a company can use the resources of the business it has taken over, which operates in a different market, to boost its market potential.

3. *The raider theory.* According to this theory, making a takeover bid to gain control of shares is a basic form of acquisition. With this method, either no negotiation has taken place between the companies involved or, if there has been any, it led nowhere. By making a public bid for shares at a fixed price (generally at a premium for the seller), one company can take control of another (at times even at the expense of paying a higher price than friendly negotiations would have generated). Although numerous theories explain this behavior, the most commonly held one is a desire to obtain rapid benefits through the synergies that can be produced. The genuine causes appear to be debt refinancing and restructuring after the sale of part of the assets of the company that is taken over. Whatever the operation's real objectives, the existing evidence (Holderness and Sheehan, 1985; Newman, Logan, and Hegarty, 1989) seems to show that a high percentage of these acquisitions or mergers have serious problems due to the excessive cost of the operation, the financial situation of the takeover company (its debt may increase to dangerous levels), and/or hostility generated in the company that is taken over. This theory is applicable to acquisitions as defined at the beginning of this chapter, but not to mergers, which must (given their very nature) be negotiated.

4. *The valuation theory.* According to this theory, acquisitions or mergers are carried out by executives who have access to more accurate information on the real value of the company to be taken over than can be found from the investment market. This information may concern advantages to be derived from the company's acquisition (e.g., operational synergies) or the fact that it has been undervalued financially. Executive opportunism plays a key role in this theory.

5. *The empire-building theory* is based on the idea that managers, who are responsible for formulating and applying strategies, have one aim in mind: to maximize their use. This is a power-based objective: the power of company management will increase as the firm achieves greater market power.

6. *The process theory* is perhaps the least developed. According to Trautwein (1990), the theory attempts to justify acquisitions and

mergers by attributing them to the limited rationale of management teams that make this decision, without bothering to carry out a deeper analysis of the alternatives.

7. *The economic disturbance theory* upholds the idea that acquisitions and mergers succeed one another in waves. They are caused by economic disturbances (Gort, 1969; Mueller, 1989) that modify individual behavior patterns and expectations. Industrial economy theories and the transaction cost theory (Williamson, 1975, 1986) form part of or are associated with this theory.

In addition to the objectives that these theories suggest company executives hope to achieve, other possible reasons are also worth mentioning, even though they do not form part of the said theories. We are referring to tax incentives and market globalization, which introduce new variables to the type of growth strategy to choose. Tax incentives (Auerbach and Reishus, 1988) can add to the benefits of an acquisition or merger, either because the acquisition is carried out using methods of finance that involve tax exemptions, or because resources from one company are transferred to another, thus reducing the payment of taxes.

A global analysis of the theories outlined, each motivated by one or several different factors, indicates that probably not just one but a combination of factors are involved in the decision to adopt this kind of strategy. Also, there is an interrelation between the different theories commented on, with the existence of mutual influences. For instance the theory by which company managers carry out a merger or an acquisition to increase their power is in turn associated with the efficiency theory, which assumes a link between the merger or acquisition and an increase in the company's efficiency (e.g., in its performance), and with the monopoly theory, in the sense that company management increases its power by increasing the company's market power or by generating synergies. Consequently, the final decision is often influenced by a combination of several of the previous reasons.

The next question is: why don't companies choose another strategic option instead, such as a *joint venture*? The answer to this question is long and complex, given that several explanations are possible and most of them are only partial answers. A plausible explanation is as follows: When the assets to be acquired are proportionate to a high percentage of the company's value and are inseparably linked to it, an acquisition or merger is the best alternative. In other cases, if complementary technologies are to be shared, for example, a joint venture is better. In fact, for each particular situation, the conditions under which the operation is to be carried out and the consequences deriving from the final decision must be analyzed.

With a merger or acquisition strategy, a series of factors must be taken into account, i.e., factors concerning the impact that this strategy will have on the human resources of the companies involved in the process, from management to operational levels. If the people affected by the decision are not informed or motivated to accept the situation, in an attempt to encourage them to react positively during the subsequent adaptation process, the operation's success will very likely be limited, if not canceled out. Another point to consider is the need for an accurate valuation of the company that is to be taken over or merged.

Finally, what implications and advantages does an acquisition-based growth strategy have for hotel companies?

- By taking over a company, the acquirer will have extended geographic coverage and/or new brand names. These will allow the acquirer to achieve its growth objectives, become a stronger presence in the hotel industry, widen its range of markets or market segments, and obtain strategic complementary businesses and the opportunity to boost its competitive advantages by incorporating new ones.
- The sector's more dynamic hotel companies seek continuously to increase their market share, so as to achieve economies of scale in fields such as bookings, information technologies, marketing, and purchases. In short, the objective is to acquire resources and abilities that the company either lacks or which it cannot make optimum use of, because it is not the right size to do so.
- Increasingly clients expect their hotel company to provide a service that includes worldwide discounts and hotel coverage in most cities, with a level of quality that meets their expectations.
- Also, a study by Kim and Olsen (1999) reflects the importance of a company's increased value within the hotel industry, from the perspective of its shares, together with the fact that mergers

are seen as a way of increasing the company's capacity at a lower cost than if it were to extend its facilities or acquire more tangible assets.[1]

EXAMPLES

One of the international hotel industry's most significant events is the wave of mergers and acquisitions that it has experienced, leading to radical changes in competition. According to Myro (1999), if direct investment into a specific industry is carried out through mergers and acquisitions, the causes are very closely linked with the need for the restructuring of the business and its products, processes, markets, and locations, within the framework of an increasingly competitive environment. As the hotel industry expands globally, mergers and acquisitions are becoming more and more popular. The acquisition-based growth strategies used by some hotel chains since the early 1990s have been caused by the following.

The first factor is the shortage of possible locations for hotels, high building costs, and the need for strategic market locations. Indeed, in tourism and more particularly in the hotel business, the location of a company's premises is clearly a key asset that determines its business success. Due to the lack of available land that characterizes some destinations, the acquisition of existing accommodation is one of the more commonly used forms of hotel expansion.

In addition, companies' improved ability to raise finance and the hotel industry's sound stock market performance (Whitford, 1998) have both acted as the driving forces behind this trend, in consonance with "Merton's conjecture," which defends reductions in the cost of company capital as the number of shareholders increases. Also, the accommodation industry's increasing interest in big property investment trusts has acted as the incentive for this process of concentration. The protagonists of two of the most significant takeovers to have taken place in the past few years were two real estate investment trusts (REITs)[2] with "paired share" status: a company status in the United States that offers certain tax benefits in comparison with other forms of company, thus allowing the former to pay higher prices in company acquisitions.[3] Non-REIT hotel companies such as Hilton Hotels Corporation and Marriott International, known as C-corps, lobbied the U.S. government about these unfair tax breaks and the loophole was closed in 1998, bringing the wave of consolidation to an end. U.S. companies were only just beginning to make forays overseas, driven, to a certain extent, by an absence of opportunities in North America. In the end, however, only the United Kingdom's Arcadian group fell to a paired-share REIT in the form of Patriot American Hospitality.

Last, an empirical study of mergers and acquisitions in the U.S. hotel industry (Kim and Olsen, 1999) shows that, although the consolidation process that the industry underwent in the early 1990s was caused by a desperate effort to cut costs through business restructuring processes, the industry's recent wave of acquisitions and mergers is mainly attributable to growth objectives.

The U.S. hotel trade is one of the industries that has been most actively involved in acquisitions, and membership of hotel chains has become almost compulsory practice. In Europe, where independent hotels still predominate, this trend is yet to reach the same scope or magnitude,[4] although news is beginning to filter through of some operations, such as those involving Spanish companies. Table 7.1 shows the most representative examples of this worldwide trend, indicating the magnitude of this phenomenon in the hotel industry.

In comparison with previous years, the years 1998 to 2000 saw something of a deal drought in the United States. This was due to the sharp downturn in the share prices of accommodation companies. Although hotel companies worldwide suffered if they were listed companies, the U.S. situation was particularly marked, with many companies suffering a halving or worse in their share prices. Apart from Hilton Hotels Corporation's acquisition of Promus in 1999, a deal that owners of Hilton Hotels Corporation were desperate to conclude, having failed to buy ITT Sheraton, there have been no other major acquisitive deals by publicly quoted U.S.-based operating companies during the three years (1998-2000). Instead, the deals have been either by private equity or European operators. The deals that have been completed in the United States have mostly been about restructuring, particularly the sale of hotel property assets with or without management contracts to tidy up balance sheets and brand portfolios.

TABLE 7.1. The Accommodation Industry—Mergers and Acquisitions, 2000-1993

Date	Acquirer	Acquired	$ (Millions)
2000	Whitbread	Swallow	937.8
2000	NH Hoteles	Krasnapolsky	463.1
2000	Occidental	Allegro	400
2000	Sol Meliá	Tryp	344.4
2000	Barceló	Hampstead Group	325
2000	Starwood Hotels & Resorts	Ciga SpA	295
2000	Pandox	Hotellus International	247
2000	FINOVA Group/Pitney Bowes	Accor	189
2000	Six Continents PLC	SPHC	183.3
2000	London Vista	Regal	177.9
2000	Six Continents PLC	Bristol Hotels & Resorts, Inc.	157
2000	Grupo Fusi	Bonaparte	146.5
2000	Mandarin Oriental	Rafael	142.5
2000	Hospitality Ventures LLC	Prime Hospitality	112
2000	MWB	Wyndham	111.5
2000	Hospitality Properties Trust	Marriott International	109.1
2000	Lee Hing Developments	Colony Capital	102
2000	Pierre et Vacances	Gran Dorado	96.3
2000	RLJ Development LLC	Hilton Hotels Corporation	95
2000	Accor	Privatization	74.9
2000	Scandic	Provobis	70.6
2000	Airtours	Don Pedro	66.5
2000	London & Regional	Premier Hotels	66.1
2000	Premier Hotels	Oriel	58.8
2000	De Vere Hotels	Bringemere	51.6
2000	Hanover International	Andrew Weir	50
2000	CNL Hospitality Properties	Wyndham International	43.4

TABLE 7.1 *(continued)*

Date	Acquirer	Acquired	$ (Millions)
2000	Airtours	Hotetur Club	40.3
2000	Accor	Thakral Holdings	18.5
2000	Choice Hotels Scandinavia	Beyer & Kjaer	17.8
2000	Danubius	Lecebne	14.4
2000	TAHL	Rest Inn	9.3
1999	Hilton	Promus	4,000
1999	Hilton	Stakis	1,875.8
1999	Ladbroke PLC	Stakis	1,819
1999	Accor	Red Roof Inns	1,100
1999	Millennium & Copthorne	CDL Hotels International	899
1999	SHP Acquisition LLC	Sunstone Hotel Investors Inc.	880
1999	Shangri-La Asia Ltd.	Shangri-La Hotels Companies	642.7
1999	Millennium & Copthorne	Richfield Hospitality Services	640
1999	Millennium & Copthorne	Regal Hotels International	640
1999	LaSalle Partners Inc.	Jones Lang Wootton	540
1999	Accor/Colony Capital/ Blackstone	Vivendi	493.5
1999	Westmont	UniHost Corporation	377
1999	Starwood Hotel & Resorts	Vistana Inc.	360
1999	Jurys	Doyle	334.7
1999	Accor	Société National du Ferrocarnlé (SNFC)	247.4
1999	Regal Hotel Group	County	194
1999	Marriott International	ExecuStay Corporation	128
1999	Hand Picked Hotels	Arcadian International	120
1999	Hand Picked Hotels	Wyndham	112
1999	Norwich Union	Hilton	111.3
1999	Jameson Inns	Signature Inns	105.1
1999	Hampshire Hotels and Resorts	Loews Corp. NY	101

TABLE 7.1 *(continued)*

Date	Acquirer	Acquired	$ (Millions)
1999	Golden Tulip	Servico	100.2
1999	Zenith HI Investors	Promus Hotel Corp.	99.8
1999	Choice Hotels Scandina-via	Choice Properties	99.4
1999	Promociones Eurobuilding SA	Shuaa Hotels	84.4
1999	Sol Meliá	Boutique Properties	80.9
1999	Starwood Hotel & Resorts Worldwide Inc.	Moriah Hotels	74.4
1999	Hospitality Property Trust	Sholodge	65
1999	Golden Tulip	AMEV	64.2
1999	Alchemy Partners/Para-mount Hotels	Scottish Highland Ho-tels PLC	61
1999	Paramount	Scottish Highland	60.8
1999	Accor SA	SA Hotels de Bourgogne	57.1
1999	Vail Resorts, Inc.	Grand Teton Lodge Company	50
1999	Humphrey Hospitality Trust, Inc.	Supertel Hospitality, Inc.	43.3
1999	Hand Picked Hotels	Virgin Group	34
1999	Grand Hotel Group	Rank Group	32.3
1999	Accor	J. Chister Ericsson Family	22.6
1999	Golden Tulip	Alfa	19.2
1999	Kransapolsky Hotels and Restaurants	Alfa Group	19
1999	Lane Hospitality Northbrook	Prime Hospitality	17
1999	Jacob Development Ann Arbor	Sunburst Hospitality Corp.	15
1999	Peel	Grace	14
1999	Regis Hotel Corp.	Wilmont Ltd.	11.8
1999	Kransapolsky Hotels and Restaurants	European Hotels Ven-tures	8.1
1999	Groupe Envergure	Groupe de l'Hotellerie	8

TABLE 7.1 *(continued)*

Date	Acquirer	Acquired	$ (Millions)
1999	Suburban Lodges of America	GuestHouse International LLC	3.3
1999	Accor SA	Premiere Lodge	undisclosed
1999	Canadian Pacific Ltd.	67% stake of Fairmont Hotel Management L.P.	undisclosed
1999	Luxe Worldwide Hospitality	Robert F. Warner Distinguished Hotels	undisclosed
1999	Westmont Hospitality/ Whitehall	Cronos Hotel SpA	undisclosed
1999	Pierre et Vacances	Westmont	undisclosed
1999	Westmont	ENI	undisclosed
1999	Westmont Hospitality/ Whitehall	Agiforte International Spa	undisclosed
1999	Westmont	Paribas	undisclosed
1998	Starwood Lodging Trust	ITT Corp.	14,600
1998	CapStar	American General Hospitality	3,000
1998	Six Continents PLC	InterContinental	2,900
1998	Six Continents PLC	Saison	2,850
1998	The Meditrust Companies	La Quinta Inns, Inc.	2,650
1998	Patriot American Hospitality Inc.	Interstate Hotels Corp.	2,100
1998	FelCor Suite Hotels	Bristol Hotel Company	1,900
1998	FelCor Suite Hotels	Bristol Hotels	1,700
1998	Starwood Lodging Trust	Westin Hotels & Resorts	1,570
1998	Patriot American Hospitality Inc.	Wyndham Hotel Corp.	1,100
1998	Blackstone	Granada	879.1
1998	Blackstone Hotel Acquisition Co.	Saboy Hotels	866
1998	Canadian Pacific	Century	674.7
1998	Canadian Pacific	Princess Hotel	540.3
1998	Canadian Pacific	Lonrho	540
1998	Servico	Impac	538

TABLE 7.1 *(continued)*

Date	Acquirer	Acquired	$ (Millions)
1998	American General Hosp.	CapStar	530
1998	Patriot American Hospitality	Carnival Hotels & Resorts	485
1998	Whitehall Street Real Estate LLP	Chartwell Leisure Inc.	348.5
1998	Patriot American Hospitality Inc.	WHG Resorts & Casinos Inc.	300
1998	Patriot American Hospitality Inc.	Arcadian International	296
1998	Boykin Lodging Company	Red Lion Inns Limited Partnership	271
1998	American General Hosp.	Financial Security Assurance	270
1998	FelCor Lodging Trust	Starwood	243
1998	Patriot	Arcadian	206.3
1998	Patriot American Hospitality Inc.	Summerfield Hotel Corp.	180
1998	Hilton Hotels	Yarmouth Group	168
1998	Kransapolsky	Golden Tourism International	152
1998	Intrawest Corporation	Sandestin Resorts, Inc.	130
1998	Credit Suisse First Boston	Gotham Hospitality Group	130
1998	Grupo Posadas	Caesars Park Hotels	123
1998	Peel financed by Lehman Brothers	Thistle	111.6
1998	Destination Europe	Cliveden	104.2
1998	Westmont	QMH	103.1
1998	Bristol Hotel Co.	Omaha Hotel Inc.	100
1998	Grand Hotel Group	Australian Tourism Group	100
1998	Scandic	Arctia	95
1998	Servico	City Hotels	87.6
1998	US Franchise Systems	Best Inns & Suites	84
1998	Canadian Pacific	Delta Hotels & Resorts	66.7
1998	Alchemy Partners	ASB Group	62.7
1998	Walton Milan Investors	Regent Milano Spa	61.5

TABLE 7.1 *(continued)*

Date	Acquirer	Acquired	$ (Millions)
1998	Promus Hotel Corp.	Harrison Conference Associates, Inc.	60
1998	Norwich Union	Lyric Hotels	58.5
1998	Realty Refund Trust	InnSuites Hotels	57.6
1998	Paramount	Granada	55.8
1998	Investor Group	Seoul Miramar Corp.	51.4
1998	Janus Hotels and Resorts	The Cornerstone Group	44.1
1998	Swallow	Manor Hotels	33.9
1998	Vaux Group	Manor Hotels	33
1998	Norwich Union	West Fonds	28
1998	Signature Resorts	MMG Holding, MMG Development Corporations	26.5
1998	Canadian Hotel Income	Sea Tac	21.4
1998	Movenpick Holding	Karos Hotels	15
1998	Rica	City Hotels Holding AB	8
1998	Sol Meliá	Zagrebacka Bank & Barrington Hotels & Resorts	5
1998	Radisson Hotel Worldwide	DC International	3
1998	Capitol Communities Corporation	Entry Resorts	1
1998	Beijing Enterprise Holdings	Jianguo International Hotels	undisclosed
1998	CapStar	Metro Hotels	undisclosed
1998	MeriStar	South Seas Properties	undisclosed
1998	Aqua Pia Antica Marcia	Banco de Sicilia	undisclosed
1998	Accor	Postiljon	undisclosed
1998	Scandic	Finest Hotel Company	undisclosed
1998	Rica	North Cape Hotels AS	undisclosed
1998	Corinthia Hotels	Top Spirit	undisclosed
1998	Agip Spa	Agip Forte International Hotels	undisclosed
1998	ENI	Agip Forte International Hotels	undisclosed
1997	Promus Hotel Corp.	Doubletree Corporation	4,700

TABLE 7.1 *(continued)*

Date	Acquirer	Acquired	$ (Millions)
1997	Marriott Inc.	Renaissance	1,000
1997	Host Marriott Corp.	Forum Group Inc.	540
1997	Starwood Lodging Trust	Flatley Company/Tara Hotels	470
1997	Starwood Lodging Trust	HEI Hotels LLC	327
1997	Sunstone Hotel Investors	Kahler Realty Corporation	322
1997	Extended Stay America	Studio Plus	290
1997	Patriot American Hospitality Inc.	Resorts LLP/Carefree Resorts Corp./Resort Services, Inc.	256.6
1997	Sino Land and Sino Hotels	Greenroll	245.5
1997	Fairfield Communities Inc.	Vacation Break USA Inc.	240
1997	Patriot American Hospitality Inc.	California Jockey Club and Bay Meadows Operating Company	238.6
1997	West Hospitality Group	Orion	210.1
1997	Wyndham Hotel Corp.	ClubHouse Hotels Inc.	130
1997	Prime Hospitality	Homegate Hospitality Inc.	125
1997	Corporation Financiera Reunida	NH Hoteles	101
1997	Intrawest Corporation	Whistle Mountain Holdings	85.8
1997	Elegant Hotels	St. James Beach Hotels	73.5
1997	Signature Resorts Inc.	Plantation Resorts Group	59.1
1997	Danubius	Hungar Hotels	52.6
1997	Signature Resorts, Inc.	LSI Group Holdings PLC	50.6
1997	Tokay Kanco	Tres Malaysian, 3 British Real Estate	43.9
1997	CapStar Hotel Company	Winston Hospitality, Inc.	34
1997	Host Marriott Corp.	Chesapeake Hotel Limited Partnership	31.5
1997	Signature Resorts, Inc.	Vacation Internationale, Ltd.	24.3

TABLE 7.1 *(continued)*

Date	Acquirer	Acquired	$ (Millions)
1997	Bau Holdings Age	Warsaw-Syrena Hotel Chaine	24
1997	Vistana, Inc.	The Success Companies and Points of Colorado	24
1997	Patriot American Operating Company	Grand Heritage Hotels	22
1997	Signature Resorts, Inc.	AVCOM International	21.6
1997	Grupo Acerero del Norte	50% of Quinta Real	20
1997	Signature Resorts, Inc.	Global Development Ltd.	18
1997	Signature Resorts, Inc.	Marc Hotels & Resorts, Inc.	6
1997	Carlson Travel Group	Wagonlit	undisclosed
1997	Swissotel Management	Swiss International Hotels	undisclosed
1996	Doubletree Corporation	Red Lion Hotels	1,174.1
1996	HFS	Resort Condominiums International (time-share company)	825
1996	Bristol	61 Holiday Inns purchased from Six Continents PLC	659
1996	Marriott International	Forum Group Inc.	605
1996	Stakis PLC	Metropole Hotels	534
1996	TRT Holdings Inc.	Omni Hotels Group	500
1996	FelCor Suite Hotels	Crown Sterling Suites	325
1996	Hilton	Prudential Insurance's interest in four upscale Hiltons	267
1996	Hilton Hotels	5% stake in Ladbroke Group PLC	190
1996	National Lodging Corporation	Ownership interest in 96 Travelodge motels from Forte PLC	98
1996	Janola Dale Property Ltd.	Dreamworld Corp.	63
1996	RIU Hotels	Ascot Holdings' Spanish Hotels Business	62.5

TABLE 7.1 *(continued)*

Date	Acquirer	Acquired	$ (Millions)
1996	Doubletree Corporation	Hotel mgmt. company RFS Inc.	58.1
1996	National Lodging Corporation	Acquired majority interest in Chartwell Leisure	57
1996	Interstate	The mgmt. company associated with Equity Inns	46.5
1996	HFS	Travelodge Hotel trademark and franchise from Forte PLC	39.3
1996	Motels of America	Ownership of 19 Travelodge Motels from Forte PLC	32
1996	Doubletree Corporation	Interest in the REIT RFS Hotel Investors	18.5
1996	Republic Hotels	PT Tanahabang India Pratama	13.8
1996	Glynhill International	51% of Partnership with Century International	11.9
1996	North American Resorts Inc.	Voyageur First Inc.	undisclosed
1995	United/Harvey Holdings LP	United Inns	537
1995	Lane Hospitality	Victor Management	347.8
1995	Marriott International	49% interest in Ritz-Carlton	200
1995	Starwood Capital Group	Westin Hotels	153.4
1995	HFS	Knights Inn franchise system	undisclosed
1995	Club Mediterranee SA	Club Med Inc.	116.9
1995	FelCor Suite Hotels	Crown Sterling Suites acq. 6 hotels and franchises	66.6
1995	CDL Hotels International	Copthorne Hotels Holdings	15
1995	Mabuhay Holdings	Filipine Plaza Holdings	2.5
1994	Forte PLC	57.3% of Société des Hotels Meridies	202.7

TABLE 7.1 *(continued)*

Date	Acquirer	Acquired	$ (Millions)
1994	Indemnity Holdings	Star of Cripple Creek Casino	179
1994	Forte PLC	Société des Hotels Meridies	137.3
1994	Investor Group	Santa Fe Financial Corp. (own and operate hotels)	110
1994	Sea Containers Ltd.	Orient-Express Hotels Inc.	75.2
1994	Powder Corporation	Alpine Meadows of Tahoe	38.2
1994	Doubletree Corporation	Guest Quarters Suites	20
1994	Mr. Macal	Mortaix de Portugal Investmentos Hoteleiros	15
1994	HFS	Villager Lodge franchise system	5
1994	Intrawest Corporation	Stratton Ski/Victoria USA Inc.	undisclosed
1994	Buckhead America	Crickett Inn limited motel franchise system from Salomon Brothers	undisclosed
1993	New World Development	Stouffer Hotels	1,000
1993	Morgan Stanley	Red Roof Inns	637
1993	ITT Sheraton	Desert Inn Properties	160
1993	HFS	Super 8 Motels	125
1993	Choice Hotels International	Journey's End	10
1993	HFS	Park Inns	5

Source: Ader, J.N., La Fleur, R.A., Yurman, J.J., and McCoy, T. (2000). *Global lodging almanac.* New York: Bear Stearns.

The protagonists of the year 2000 were European hotel chains, specifically Spanish ones. Whitbread, NH Hoteles, Occidental, Sol Meliá, and Barceló signed agreements for the year's five most expensive takeovers. These five acquisitions represented about half the cost of the hotel industry's total acquisitions for the entire year 2000.

Whitbread,[5] a company owning the property rights of the Marriott International brand name in the United Kingdom, bought the entire share capital[6] of Swallow Hotels, amounting to 938 million dollars. The profile of Swallow hotels (four-star-type hotels in the United Kingdom's leading cities) complements the group's London properties. With this deal, Whitbread became the second biggest hotel operator in the United Kingdom, surpassed only by Six Continents PLC.

Over the past few years, the most expensive acquisitions have been ITT's acquisition by Starwood Hotels & Resorts Worldwide (14.6 billion dollars), Doubletree's acquisition by Promus Hotels Corporation (4.7 billion dollars), and Promus Hotel Corporation's acquisition by Hilton Hotels Corporation (4 billion dollars). Note that the three biggest acquisitions involved U.S. chains.

The most significant year for acquisitions and mergers was 1998. During the year, almost 44 billion dollars were invested in acquisitions, meaning that more money changed hands that year than all the other years put together (1993-2000).

Recent acquisitions included Cendant Corporation's adding AmeriHost Inn to its portfolio, acquiring the brand name and franchise rights to AmeriHost Properties.

Six Continents PLC acquired Posthouse for more than 1.1 billion dollars. Posthouse has 12,300 hotel rooms in seventy-nine midrange hotels in the United Kingdom (seventy-eight premises) and Ireland (one hotel). At the end of 2000, a new hotel in Oxford was added to its hotel portfolio.

Six Continents PLC also reached an agreement to buy Hale International Limited, the owner of fifty-nine hotels in the Asian-Pacific area. The agreement included twenty-four hotels in Australia, thirteen hotels in New Zealand, nine in islands of the South Pacific, and thirteen in the rest of Asia.

In 2001, Hilton International purchased the Scandic Scandinavian hotel chain for 983 million euros. Most of the chain's 133 hotels are located in Nordic countries. Twenty Scandinavian Scandic properties were transformed into Hilton hotels, together with an additional seventeen hotels outside the region based in European cities where Hilton did not have any hotel coverage. The rest of its Scandinavian portfolio will continue operating under the Scandic brand name.

During 2000, the Accor group acquired full ownership of two Hong Kong–based hotel management groups: Century International Hotels[7] and Zenith Hotels International.[8] With this deal, Accor, which already had a 25 percent stake in Century International Hotels and a 49 percent stake in Zenith Hotels International, gained over 200 hotels in the Asian-Pacific region. All the hotels were put under the French hotel group's different brand names.

In the same year, the owners of Spanish hotel chain NH Hoteles purchased the German chain Astron.[9] More specifically, they acquired 80 percent of its share capital for a value of 130 million euros, with option rights to buy the remaining 20 percent. According to the chairmen of both companies, Astron shares many features in common with NH Hoteles: it is focused on the inner-city and business sectors, and it is positioned in the midprice, four-star hotel segment.

Sol Meliá acquired 100 percent of the share capital of Croatian Hotels & Resorts Management for the sum of 3 million dollars. The company owns twenty-one tourist accommodation properties, with a total of 16,000 accommodation units in Croatian campsites on the Istria peninsula. Sol Meliá took over 50 percent of these accommodation units, thereby becoming Croatia's leading hotel chain.

SUMMARY

This chapter explored the current wave of mergers and acquisitions that the international hotel industry experienced, because these operations have had a major effect on the tourist industry, radically changing the competitive scenario for international hotel chains. We analyzed the issue of acquisitions and mergers, both from a conceptual point of view (where we looked at key theories on mergers and acquisitions, internal versus external growth, and the pros and cons of the two strategies) and from a practical perspective. The chapter ended with an analysis of major examples of mergers and takeovers in the hotel industry between 1993 and 2000, with particular emphasis on the financial figures negotiated in 1998.

Chapter 8

Strategic Alliances: The Case of Joint Ventures

THE THEORY

A highly important phenomenon during the 1980s was the emergence of numerous different forms of intercompany cooperation or alliances. This trend will only increase in the future, an assertion that is confirmed by the long list of strategies of this kind that have been put into practice in recent years, particularly on an international level.

What is cooperation though? In general terms, cooperation can be defined as an agreement between leaders of two or more companies, who decide to act jointly in at least some of their business activities in order to achieve certain objectives. This definition, upon which we will later elaborate, means that a wide range of intercompany agreements can be classified as examples of cooperation.

Cooperation is a form of organization that differs from a market or company. Since Williamson (1975, 1986) first formulated his economic transaction cost theory, two methods have been identified for organizing the allocation of resources: markets or companies. Cooperation, however, is neither; it is a hybrid or intermediate system of organization, halfway between a market and a company, and it shares characteristics with each. In other words, it involves certain types of conduct that coincide with market behavior, exchanges between those involved in the cooperation partnership, and other exchanges characteristic of a company, all within a specific form of organization.

Intercompany agreements are a relatively old tradition. (Indeed, back in 1906, Toquiva formed alliances with other companies.) However, in the past few years or decades they have become standard practice and a solid strategic alternative to internal growth or other forms of external growth strategies, such as mergers. Why do companies adopt this type of strategy?

Many different arguments have been put forward to justify cooperation. Some reasons are general, whereas others are related to the internationalization of companies, market globalization, or the companies themselves.

The reasons that account for this boom in alliances include factors such as rapid, frequent technological change; shared know-how in order to obtain synergic benefits; a search for financial support and reduced financial risks; access to markets; and an increasingly competitive environment, particularly in mature sectors.

In addition, others factors specific to the internationalization and globalization of markets and companies: the requirements of those countries whose markets the company wishes to penetrate, and reduced risks for activities in certain countries.

- Rapid, frequent changes in technology and the increasing importance of technological innovations (given the regularity with which they occur, their repercussions, and the heavy investment that they involve) have made technology a key strategic factor. The existence of complementary technologies and their high cost is one of the factors that has led company leaders to seek alliances with other firms.
- Know-how (a specific, intangible asset, which normally cannot be disassociated from the company that owns it) can be shared by several companies or acquired by one of them. This umbrella term covers a wide range of different assets, associated with things such as research and development activities, client portfolios, market know-how, management systems, distribution systems, etc. With a cooperation partnership, employees of two or more companies can share their know-how and achieve positive synergic effects.
- Another key reason for cooperation is access to a specific country's market and, above all, multinational access, in which employees from one of the companies involved are familiar with the market that the other wishes to penetrate. This could be considered part of the previous reason, if we accept that familiarity with a market is also equivalent to know-how.

- Decision makers often search for financial support and reduced financial risks. Alliances are formed to develop new products requiring heavy investment and involving a high payback (James, 1985). In these cases, if a company is needed to help finance these projects, the result can be a cooperation agreement. Furthermore, shared financial commitments reduce the project's risks. In cases such as these, *venture capital* companies come to the forefront, because through cooperation they facilitate the development of new products and new activities.

- A more intense competitive environment, particularly in mature industries where stagnating or even reduced demand levels only aggravate the conditions in which companies are forced to compete, has made many company leaders consider some form of cooperation with their rivals, as it can reduce competition and make the companies' survival more feasible. Despite this, by cooperating, the companies' rivals will not simply disappear. Competition will continue, but under other conditions, i.e., among the companies as a whole (e.g., the organization formed as a result of the cooperation agreement and all the others that have not resorted to cooperation).

The different ways that alliance or cooperation strategies can be applied will be presented next, but first some clarifications should be made.

Literature on alliances or cooperation strategies very often associates the different forms these strategies can take with joint ventures, so that alliances and joint ventures are considered one and the same. In turn, joint ventures can be subdivided into nonequity joint ventures (i.e., alliances that involve the concession of licenses, franchises, R&D contracts, or service and marketing agreements) and equity joint ventures. In this book alliances or cooperation partnerships are umbrella terms that encompass different types of cooperation strategies. The name joint venture refers to equity joint ventures. Figure 8.1 shows different types of alliances (taken from a figure by James, 1985). Each of these alternatives is defined by a specific set of characteristics.

To analyze cooperation strategies, the process that must be followed in the adoption of a cooperation strategy, whatever type it may

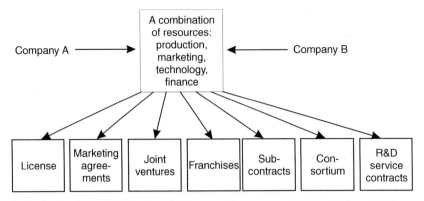

FIGURE 8.1. Alliance Strategies (Reprinted from *Long Range Planning,* 18, B.G. James, "Alliance: The new strategic focus," pp. 76-81, Copyright 1985, with permission from Elsevier.)

be, should be described. The key elements of this process are shown in Figure 8.2 (Devling and Bleackley, 1988).

The most common reasons why alliances in general and, more specifically, joint ventures tend to fail are mainly attributable to noncompliance with one or more of the points described in the alliance process.

- A poorly formulated strategy (a bad choice of partners; ambiguously defined objectives; the cooperation conditions; and/or the specific type of alliance) leads to a high percentage of failures.
- Another basic cause of failure is inefficient management of the alliance, i.e., the way in which the strategy is put into practice. Errors in the strategy's application range from inadequate structural relations between the partners or between the latter and the "daughter" company (in the case of a joint venture) to the inefficient management of the cooperation partnership.
- A third source of failure is a change in the circumstances that originally gave rise to the strategy. Changes in the goals may be sought by some of the partners involved in the alliance, causing their interest to wane and leading them to wash their hands of the alliance or call a halt to it.
- Opportunistic behavior by one of the members can end the cooperation partnership, because the other members may oppose this type of conduct and terminate the partnership.

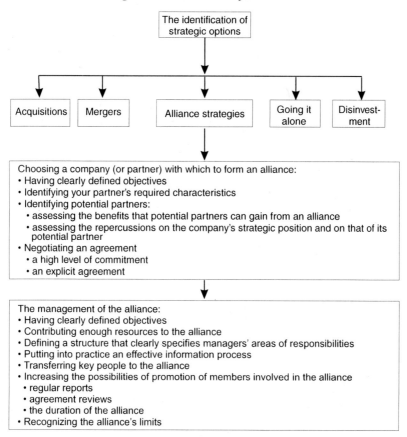

Choosing a company (or partner) with which to form an alliance:
- Having clearly defined objectives
- Identifying your partner's required characteristics
- Identifying potential partners:
  - assessing the benefits that potential partners can gain from an alliance
  - assessing the repercussions on the company's strategic position and on that of its potential partner
- Negotiating an agreement
  - a high level of commitment
  - an explicit agreement

The management of the alliance:
- Having clearly defined objectives
- Contributing enough resources to the alliance
- Defining a structure that clearly specifies managers' areas of responsibilities
- Putting into practice an effective information process
- Transferring key people to the alliance
- Increasing the possibilities of promotion of members involved in the alliance
  - regular reports
  - agreement reviews
  - the duration of the alliance
- Recognizing the alliance's limits

FIGURE 8.2. The Alliance Process (Reprinted from *Long Range Planning*, 25, G. Devling and M. Bleackley, "Strategic alliances—Guidelines for success," pp. 18-23, Copyright 1988, with permission from Elsevier.)

Last, in many cases an alliance may not be the best strategic option, so choosing this alternative may entail a high probability of failure or, at best, very poor results.

Strategic alliances range from the simplest ones (in which different hotels unite to share the same booking and marketing system) to the most complex ones, where not only hotels but also other companies join the alliance, such as travel agents, in a move toward vertical integration. The benefit of using a strategic alliance as a means of growth is that the company can swiftly take advantage of its recognition by numerous multinational companies.

Thus strategic alliances are becoming a major growth strategy for most industries, particularly the tourist industry, in which companies are becoming increasingly globalized.

Hotel chain leaders form strategic alliances in which a long-term relationship is developed, allowing them to achieve corporate goals. This type of agreement, usually reached by competitors from the same sector, is frequently termed a strategic alliance. It is defined as a long-term agreement between rival companies, which goes beyond normal market transactions without going as far as a merger (Jarillo and Martínez, 1991), or as cooperation partnerships between two or more companies in which each party seeks to increase its ability to compete by combining its resources with those of its partners (Dawson and Shaw, 1992).

Strategic alliances carried out in the hotel industry can be classified into the following three categories (Dev and Klein, 1993):

1. *One-night stands.* Short-term opportunistic relationships. These agreements are reached for publicity or promotional activities.
2. *Affairs.* Midterm operations, which can be defined as temporary unions. These relationships offer a sense of protection against competitors, so hotel chain operators tend to use them in conjunction with a small airline company or travel agency.
3. *I do.* Alliances involving a long-term commitment. More than two parties may be involved in this kind of alliance, aimed at reciprocal collaboration among the different partners. In this case a high level of cooperation is typical, as these relationships offer the possibility of considerable synergies among the parties involved.

Several advantages to using strategic alliances in the hotel trade can be found. The most important ones can be summarized as follows:

- The capacity an alliance offers to respond to consumers' changing needs
- The potentially high profits that can be obtained from extending a market geographically and from incorporating new segments

- Shared marketing costs, with broader marketing coverage, so that efforts made to achieve big economies of scale are both more effective and more efficient
- The rapid recognition of many brand names that hitherto were unknown to the market
- The minimization of many staff problems and other handicaps associated with multicultural differences, which are so common when companies seek to expand in new areas of the world

In general terms the hotel industry is undergoing an expansion process through the introduction of strategic alliances, both on an operational and strategic level. On an operational level, alliances are being formed as the sector progresses through its life cycle. On a strategic level, organizations are emerging with integrated booking systems and joint communication systems. An example of an operational alliance is what is commonly known as a "cross-franchising" operation, defined as a process in which two organizations with different products yet similar styles of management and similar company philosophies, join forces to become cost leaders by cutting costs and thereby increasing their profits.

A joint venture or equity joint venture is a type of alliance that is gaining in importance, particularly on an international level. Briefly, it involves an agreement whereby two or more legally independent companies decide to set up a firm with its own juridical status, even though it is legally owned by the parent companies (Figure 8.3). The latter dedicate part of their assets to this new company and they are rewarded with the profits that the newly created company makes.

Joint ventures can be created among companies operating in the same country (national joint ventures) or, more frequently, among companies based in different countries (international joint ventures).

Because a joint venture results in the creation of a new company, it involves much greater commitment by the firms that subscribe to this form of cooperation than other methods already described. The management team responsible for the "daughter" company is created subsequent to the joint venture agreement, plus assets are invested in the company and a series of objectives must be achieved. Consequently, any problems deriving from the mismanagement of the joint venture and those that emerge during the running of the company will have more serious repercussions. The degree of irreversibility is much higher.

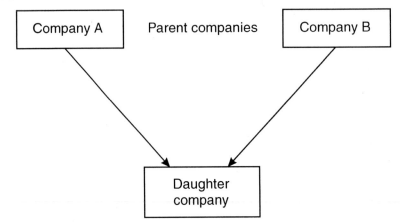

FIGURE 8.3. A Joint Venture

Joint ventures can be formed between rivals, and the venture or "daughter" company will also operate in the same market as they do. These are horizontal joint ventures. If, on the other hand, it involves a buyer and a seller or two companies from two consecutive levels of the production chain, and/or the "daughter" company operates on one of these levels, this is a vertical joint venture.

After an extensive empirical study, Harrigan (1985, 1988) established a link between the number of joint ventures or other forms of cooperation and different types of competitive environments. Figure 8.4 (Harrigan, 1988) shows the effect of an uncertain demand and the demand's growth rate when a joint venture is adopted.

An analysis of the contents of Figure 8.4 and the characteristics of different sectors (Porter, 1982) implies that joint ventures are more common in emerging or mature sectors, characterized by a very unstable demand.

This kind of strategy normally entails complex structures and negotiations, because it is usually carried out between two companies of different nationalities.

When entering into a contract of this kind, decision makers must

- specify in the contract what each party will contribute toward the joint venture;
- indicate the percentage of share capital owned by each party;

- decide on the distribution of profits;
- specify the risks undertaken by each party; and
- establish a procedure for decision making.

The foreign company will provide capital, technology, and, at times, a worldwide sales network. The other partner (the local company) will supply capital, know-how regarding the target market, and access to it. These contributions highlight the advantages that joint ventures offer for the parties involved. On one hand, the local company benefits from the financial and technological resources that the foreign company provides, which it could not develop by itself. On the other hand, the foreign company obtains access to and knowledge of the local market, investing a lower amount of capital than it would if it created its own subsidiary company, thereby reducing its risks.

The main drawbacks of joint ventures are the problems that arise due to the need to unite two cultures under the same business umbrella and company philosophy.

	A rapid increase in demand	Slow growth, stagnation, or a decrease in demand
	Many joint ventures	
A highly uncertain demand	Many vertical joint ventures in emerging markets, to reduce squeezes in stocks or to share the capacities of supply plants until a critical mass is reached	Many horizontal joint ventures, to increase the capacity of national industry and revitalize local companies involved in the joint venture
	Few joint ventures	
A demand with a low uncertainty	Many non-joint-venture cooperation agreements, aimed at attracting clients quickly or at meeting the demand for components	Few joint ventures between rival companies as a gradual means of disinvestment

FIGURE 8.4. The Effect of an Uncertain Demand and the Repercussion of the Demand's Growth Rate on the Creation of Joint Ventures (*Source:* "Joint ventures and competitive strategy," K.R. Harrigan, *Strategic Management Journal.* Copyright 1988. © John Wiley & Sons Limited. Reproduced with permission.)

The next section highlights several examples of the world's leading hotel chains that have adopted strategic alliances.

EXAMPLES

Hilton Hotels Corporation and Hilton International

Hilton Hotels Corporation and Hilton International formed a strong alliance in 1997. The two companies share the name Hilton, although each is totally different and belongs to different owners.

The name Hilton Hotels is not well-known throughout the world because of the hotels run by the American Hilton. Hilton Hotels Corporation sold Hilton International in 1964, and it was purchased three years later by TWA, together with the right to use the brand name outside the United States. Hilton Hotels Corporation retained the brand name rights within the United States, except for Hawaii, where Hilton International was allowed to keep the name of the hotel that it runs there. Since then, Hilton Hotels Corporation has operated outside the United States under the Conrad International name, using the name of the company's founder, Conrad Hilton. Because Hilton Hotels Corporation purchased Promus in 1999, with the subsequent integration of its brand names, Hilton Hotels Corporation operates in international markets with brand names other than Conrad International.[1]

The future of Hilton Hotels Corporation depends on, among other things, its alliance with Hilton International. The alliance will shape both companies' future growth. Structurally, this agreement allows each Hilton firm to acquire up to 20 percent of the other company, and also enables them to carry out joint future hotel projects. This, in itself, could give the two companies an inseparable status. The alliance has several key objectives related to marketing, growth, and the companies' branding policy:

- A company was formed for the joint worldwide promotion and development of the Hilton brand name. This includes the joint coordination and development of publicity, promotional activities, product development, and booking systems.

- Under the terms of this alliance, Hilton Hotels Corporation's frequent customer program, the prestigious Hilton HHonors (HH), was extended to include all Hilton hotels.
- Both companies can participate in the development of the other's future hotel projects. This can include a shareholding of up to 20 percent in the development of each of the other's full-service hotels, provided that the necessary capital is invested in exchange for 20 percent of the profits that the hotel then makes.
- Under an agreement between Conrad hotels and Hilton International hotels, the latter is now responsible for the future development of the Conrad brand name outside the United States for the next twenty years.
- Hilton Hotels Corporation holds the franchiser rights to the Hilton brand name in Mexico, Canada, and the island of St. John (in the U.S. Virgin Islands). This highly advantageous right will entitle Hilton International to 20 percent of the profits.
- Both companies have agreed to develop a worldwide midcategory brand name, Hilton Garden Inn.

Choice Hotels International

Choice Hotels International has formed several strategic alliances. Among these, the most important include alliances in 1997 with the British Friendly PLC,[2] the Canadian UniHost,[3] and the Australian Flag International Limited.[4]

The company is also forming several other strategic alliances so that its franchisees receive better service in matters such as tax affairs, energy, etc. For example, an alliance was formed with Grant Thornton LLP, under the terms of which this company will act as a tax consultant for Choice International Hotels' franchisees in the United States, so that they can save in the payment of state and local taxes.

Another alliance was entered into with Chevron Energy Solutions and the Tharaldson Energy Group to lower the energy costs of the company's hotels in the United States.

Another agreement was reached in 1997 with Thai Gypsum Products, which focused on hotel development. Initially it covered the Sleep Inns brand name in the Asian Pacific.

In 2001, Choice Hotels International subscribed to a joint venture with Greens, aimed at increasing its presence in Japan. Both companies formed KK Nippon Choice, which is wholly owned by Greens. The objective of the agreement is to develop the Quality and Comfort brand names in Japan. As of December 31, 2004, Comfort had sixteen hotels and Quality had two hotels.

Choice Hotels International executives signed an agreement in Asia with the leaders of the Japanese hotel company Vessel, in order to build at least twenty Sleep Inns in Asia within fifteen years.

Starwood Hotels & Resorts Worldwide and Schorghuber Corporate

In early 1998, a joint venture was started between Starwood Hotels & Resorts Worldwide and Schorghuber Corporate, leading to the creation of Arabella Sheraton. The Schorghuber Corporate group kept 51 percent of the share capital, while Sheraton obtained the remaining 49 percent. Arabella Sheraton, which is based in Munich, took charge of four Sheraton hotels and fourteen Arabella hotels in Germany, Switzerland, and Spain, together with any future projects in these countries. Arabella's objective was to consolidate and expand its hotel business. Sheraton's objective was to benefit from the positive image that the Arabella brand name has in the German market.

Cendant Corporation and Marriott International

Cendant Corporation and Marriott International have announced a joint venture for the concession of franchises in the United States for the Days Inn and Ramada brand names. This agreement means that Marriott International will pay out 205 million dollars, reserving the right to abandon the joint venture after two years.

Marriott International and Bulgari SpA

Marriott International and Bulgari SpA have signed a joint venture for the development of a coproject: a chain of luxury hotels operating under the Bulgari Hotels & Resorts brand name. The project involves initial investment of 2.131 billion dollars through 2006. During this time they hope to acquire seven hotels in Rome, Paris, and five of the world's other leading capitals. These hotels will offer a product based on carefully prepared cuisine and elegant, exclusive décor.

Six Continents and Dorint Hotels

In 2000, an alliance was formed in Germany between Six Continents and Dorint Hotels. Its objective was for Dorint Hotels to supervise the development and management of the InterContinental and Dorint brand names in certain German cities.

Sol Meliá and Iberia

Sol Meliá and Iberia Airlines subscribed to a joint venture that constituted a landmark in the history of Spanish tourism, because both companies were leaders of their respective business segments. As a result of this strategy, the tour operator Viva Tours was created, with synergies that mutually benefited both companies.

Grupo Barceló, FCC, and Argentaria

In 1998, Grupo Barceló, FCC, and Argentaria together started a joint venture, leading to the creation of Grubarges. This transaction is explained in greater detail in Chapter 6, which focuses on diagonal integration.

Accor and Amorim

Accor and its Portuguese partner, Amorim, have set in motion a plan to develop twenty-five hotels in Cuba by the year 2004. (As of June 30, 2003, it had only three hotels.) Accor has dedicated the Sofitel and Novotel brand names to this agreement, normally used for their top range of inner-city hotels. This joint venture also involves the investment of 25 million dollars in the refurbishment of the seven hotels currently operating in this Caribbean country.

Sol Meliá, Barceló, Iberostar, and Telefónica

Sol Meliá, Barceló, Iberostar, and Telefónica created Hotelnet, a B2B Internet portal for the hotel industry. Sol Meliá and Telefónica each own 24.5 percent of the shareholding, Barceló owns 10 percent, and Iberostar 8 percent. The remaining share capital was left open for possible new investors, which took the form of AC Hoteles, Fiesta,

H10, Grupo Husa, Grupo Piñero, Hesperia, Catalonia, Mac, and Med Playa.

The owners of Hotelnet intended to create a virtual marketplace for hotel owners and their suppliers in order to make their commercial relations less costly and more efficient. In the words of its promoters, this would lead to a reduction in purchase and sales prices and costs, while also making optimum use of resources and opening new markets. However, as of the publication time of this book, Hotelnet was in bankruptcy.

Sa Nostra, Ibercaja, Caixa Galicia, and C&N

The saving banks Sa Nostra, Ibercaja, and Caixa Galicia formed an alliance with Condor & Neckerman (C&N) to create the investment company Inversora de Hoteles Vacacionales SA, which is expected to invest 300 million euros through 2006 in the purchase or sale of tourist accommodation, primarily in Spanish tourist resorts. This new company was created with a capital of 22.2 million euros, 40 percent of which was provided by C&N and 20 percent by each of the three finance companies. The Iberostar chain, one of C&N's partners, is responsible for the management of the company's property.

Grupotel and TUI

The Grupotel hotel chain and the German tour operator TUI entered into an alliance that led to the creation of Grupotel II. This new company, with a share capital of 78 million euros (half of which was provided by each of the two partners), is responsible for running twenty-nine of the chain's thirty-three hotels, which are all located in the Balearic Islands. TUI provided its share (39 million euros) in cash, whereas Grupotel transferred the ownership of two of its hotels, Parc Natural and Gran Vista, valued as being worth the same amount of money.

SUMMARY

Alliances or cooperation can be defined as an agreement between two or more companies whose owners decide to act jointly in at least some of their business activities in order to achieve certain objectives. In the past decade the number of strategic alliances has grown exponentially, which is why this business phenomenon was explored in depth. More specifically, in this chapter we analyzed possible motives, processes, and forms of alliances. The theory section concluded by looking at the case of joint ventures. Major examples of strategic alliances by hotel chains were described, including an alliance formed in 1997 between Hilton Hotels Corporation and Hilton International, two totally different companies with different owners.

Chapter 9

Franchise Contracts

THE THEORY

Franchising is a form of cooperation between companies in which one company, the *franchiser,* grants other companies, the *franchisees,* the right to commercialize certain types of products and/or services in exchange for some kind of financial compensation. The franchise contract includes at minimum (1) the use of a shared name and a common layout, design, and presentation for the premises where the franchisees run their businesses; (2) shared know-how; and (3) ongoing technical and commercial support, given to the franchisees by the franchiser.

The concept of franchising goes back to the Middle Ages, when the Catholic Church granted franchises to tax collectors in exchange for a percentage of the money they collected. In the mid-nineteenth century, Singer became the first North American company to use franchising as a means of distributing its products (Kinch and Hayes, 1986).

During North America's economic development and the industrial revolution, franchising was used increasingly as a sales system. Back then franchising involved only a license to carry out sales of products made by a specific manufacturer. Since the 1960s this kind of franchise system, known as *product franchising,* has experienced a slight reduction in the revenue it generates, even though initially it was very widely used.[1]

Whereas brand or product franchising is becoming much less popular, *business-format franchising* is spiraling.[2] This kind of franchising system is used for operations in which the relationship between the franchiser and the franchisee not only involves the franchiser's products and services, but also a global commercial strategy that includes marketing programs, staff training, operational manuals, quality controls, standards, and ongoing fluid communication[3] (IFA, 1991; Naisbitt Group, 1989).

Franchising is often described as "a way of entering a business, but not going it alone," as it allows franchisees to join a business whose concept has already been tried and tested. With business-format franchising, the business entrepreneur is able to benefit from a fully designed commercial strategy before starting the business.

Another kind of franchising operation worth mentioning is *conversion franchising*. This is an option open to existing businesses, through which they can transform their business into a kind of sales point or "subsidiary" for a parent company. By choosing this alternative, independent business owners are able to benefit from a series of advantages, such as a greater marketing impact, a constant process of modernization, and consumer recognition[4] (IFA, 1991; Naisbitt Group, 1989).

The hotel industry was one of the pioneers in the introduction of the franchise system. With it, new hotels and other existing ones were transferred to chains' own brand names. With a hotel franchise contract, the franchisee operates under the same brand image and with the same production methods as its parent hotel chain, the franchiser. The franchiser company must be a prestigious hotel chain, with a reputation for the quality of the service its hotels provide and, as a result, a good corporate image.

A franchise contract is usually subscribed to for a period of twenty to thirty years for a fixed annual amount. The expiry can be extended if both parties are satisfied with their mutual collaboration. Nevertheless, employees from the franchising company carry out regular inspections to check full compliance with its corporate regulations and with the production process. Noncompliance with one or both aspects is sufficient for a breach of contract to be alleged, on the grounds that the hotel may discredit the franchiser.

Franchise contracts are inevitably designed to benefit the franchiser, as they are aimed at maintaining high quality controls and strict global control of the hotel product. In some cases, the franchiser will insist that the hotel is a newly built one, designed according to its own specifications. In other cases, the franchiser will give a franchise to an existing hotel, whenever the property can be converted to conform to the franchiser's requirements.

The franchiser must be in a good financial position. The hotel chain must be carefully selected, because the relationship between both parties will be long term. Ideal franchisers must have extensive experience, a successful history, and an excellent financial reputation.

Franchise strategies can be as simple as a franchiser offering a contract to one small company with a single accommodation unit. Alternatively, a franchise strategy can be as complex as master franchising, in which a company is entitled to develop a specific brand name throughout a particular region of the world.

Apart from offering initial assistance to franchisees, hotel franchisers also offer a system of finance for the business and consultancy in the design and construction of hotels. In addition, they also offer booking services, public relations assistance, quality control programs, publicity campaigns, marketing programs, and other services to help their franchisees.

One of the first hotel chains to introduce franchise contracts was Holiday Inn. This chain, which was a pioneer in the construction of U.S. hotels in the 1950s, gradually expanded by opening roadside motels in key locations and commercial centers. The philosophy was to aim for rapid growth, so franchise contracts were introduced, since a takeover strategy would have been much slower, given that it is very costly.

By no means is it easy to select a particular franchising system. One of the main points to take into account is the product. Target markets must be studied in order to carry out a subsequent analysis of the type of product that might meet potential consumers' needs. The hotel industry offers a wide range of products adapted to suit the different needs of today's tourists. After the franchisee has chosen a particular product, he or she must look for a hotel chain with a brand name that covers that particular segment. Potential franchisees will start this search by requesting information from each hotel chain they are interested in. This information must be carefully analyzed and contrasted with that of other chains so as to make the best possible choice.

Both the franchisee and the franchiser will commit themselves to mutual assessments. The former must study sample contracts and sales documentation, as well as asking many questions about the company[5] (Kinch and Hayes, 1986; Arnold, 1987; James, 1987; Mandigo, 1987; Kaplan, 1987; Lowell and Kirsch, 1991).

If someone obtains a hotel franchise and becomes a member of the business, he or she will acquire several responsibilities, such as compliance with the chain's quality control standards and participation in compulsory marketing programs, among others. Noncompliance with the hotel chain's policy in matters such as these will endanger the continuation of the franchise contract, with negative repercussions on the chain's global public image and on the value of the brand name.

A hotel franchise contract offers a series of advantages and disadvantages for both the franchiser and the franchisee.

Advantages and Disadvantages for the Franchiser

Advantages

- The franchiser earns a fixed amount by charging royalties.
- The franchiser can expand and internationalize the hotel product, thus promoting greater familiarity of the brand name, while avoiding the high financial commitments that takeovers involve.
- The opportunity to increase sales and marketing activities in target markets on both a national and an international level is possible without prohibitive costs.
- The franchiser is actively involved in the business and therefore is highly motivated to increase the business turnover.
- The operating costs of a computerized booking system can be shared proportionally by a large number of hotels.

Disadvantages

- The franchisee may fail to comply with sufficient quality controls, neglecting the hotel and permitting a decrease in the quality of its service, thus damaging the hotel chain's reputation. For this reason, franchisers must carry out inspections to check the quality of both the service offered and the product.
- Rivalry could exist between the franchiser and franchisee.

- The high cost of the initial introduction of a franchise system is sometimes prohibitive.
- An optimum choice must be made when selecting franchisees.
- The transparency of the results submitted by the franchisee may be questionable.

Advantages and Disadvantages for the Franchisee

Advantages

- Working with operational procedures that have already been tried and tested (i.e., the know-how that will be introduced in the hotel) brings peace of mind. This means that the franchisee becomes the owner of a veteran business, thereby reducing the risk that starting a new business involves.[6]
- An internationally recognized brand identity positions the hotel in the market as a member of a well-known hotel chain.
- The franchisee is connected to a booking system that is linked to the global distribution systems (GDSs) developed by airlines.
- The franchiser supports sales, marketing, and public relations activities, because if clients find fault with one of the franchisee hotels, they will associate it with the entire hotel chain.
- The franchiser provides support in staff's professional training.
- Expert advice on the introduction and application of new technologies is offered.
- Economies of scale due to centralized purchasing systems benefit the franchisee's bottom line.
- The franchisee benefits from participation in large-scale client loyalty schemes and other marketing programs.
- Customer care is based on information compiled by the chain's other hotels.
- Quality control standards and supervised procedures are guaranteed.
- A reservations phone line in several of the world's countries is free.
- Advice on financial management is provided.
- Advice on the location of properties is provided.

Disadvantages

- The high cost of franchising fees means that the RevPAR (revenue per available room) must be increased to offset these payments.
- In addition to staff training, a considerable initial investment is needed to convert the hotel or build one to conform to the franchiser's standards and requirements.
- Readapting the building to a new alternative franchise contract if the agreement with the former hotel chain should come to an end is difficult and costly.
- The franchiser's bankruptcy could lead to the winding up of the business.
- The hotel loses its own individual identity.

In exchange for the numerous advantages that a franchisee can benefit from when subscribing to a franchise contract, the franchiser requests the payment of high franchising fees. In many cases, after staff costs, these are the second biggest expenses that most franchisees face.

Traditional hotel franchising fees can be broken down as follows:

An *initial fee:* usually a fixed sum per room. This fee covers the cost of an analysis of the existing or potential hotel and expenses incurred prior to the hotel's inauguration.

A *yearly fee:* usually a percentage of the gross room revenue in exchange for the use of brand names, logos, and graphic material.

A *marketing fee:* based on a percentage of the gross room revenue. This fee helps finance the chain's promotional activities on a global level.

A *reservation fee:* usually a fixed amount for each booking made. Commissions paid to sales agents and fees for the use of GDSs must also be considered. The latter are generally regarded as the central booking system's operational costs.

Other *variable fees* might be charged to cover various different backup services, such as staff training.

The fees that franchisers charge are linked to the revenue received per room, so these sums increase very rapidly when a hotel's finances improve.

EXAMPLES

Table 9.1 shows the hotel trade's Top 10 franchisers for 2002. Almost 80 percent of the Top 10 franchisers' hotel portfolios are run under franchise contracts. North American hotel chains have invested most heavily in the franchise system. For the chains shown in the table, franchising is the main growth strategy, except for the French hotel chain Accor, which concentrates primarily on leasing contracts.

The Top 10 list of franchisers includes three hotel chains that are *pure franchisers* (i.e., 100 percent of their hotel portfolio is run through franchise contracts). These chains are Cendant Corporation, Choice Hotels International, and U.S. Franchise Systems.

TABLE 9.1. Companies That Franchise the Most Hotels, 2002

Franchiser	Total Hotels	Number Franchised	Percentage (%) Franchised
Cendant Corporation	6,624	6,624	100
Choice Hotels International	4,545	4,545	100
Six Continents Hotels	3,274	2,767	85
Hilton Hotels Corporation	1,986	1,612	81
Marriott International	2,398	1,482	62
Carlson Hospitality Worldwide	788	758	96
Accor	3,654	757	21
U.S. Franchise Systems	500	500	100
Société du Louvre	933	409	44
Tharaldson Enterprises	341	340	99.7

Source: www.hostelmag.com.

The hotel chains that have undergone the highest international growth are the ones that have concentrated most heavily on the franchising system. Indeed, the world's seven biggest franchisers are also the world's seven biggest hotel chains in terms of rooms. Therefore, a hotel chain's growth strategy is directly proportionate to its position in the ranks of the world's hotel industry. This explains the big differences between the portfolios of North American and European hotel chains such as Riu, Iberostar, and Barceló, as the latter have based their growth strategies mainly on hotel ownership.

Franchise contracts involve a lower investment risk and a reduced cyclical risk for businesses in comparison with property ownership. Indeed, in the case of property ownership, if a hotel has had a bad season with low occupancy figures and a loss is made, the owner incurs the loss. In contrast, with franchise contracts, even if negative results are obtained one season, the franchiser will still make a profit. This is because, with the fee system, the franchiser charges a fixed percentage based on the number of hotel rooms and another fixed amount dependent on the hotel turnover.

Cendant Corporation

Cendant Corporation is the world's largest franchising chain and the one with the greatest number of rooms in the world. Cendant Corporation is a pure franchising company. This means that its entire portfolio operates under a franchise system, so it owns no hotels at all. Its aim is to provide services for its franchisees so that they can increase their room occupancy rates and productivity levels. To do this, Cendant leaders offer backup services including marketing campaigns on national and regional levels, staff training, a strict quality control system for its franchisee hotels, a free telephone booking system for clients (which is very popular with the latter), a system of financial assistance for hotel owners consisting of a cash-flow analysis (called the Cost Tumbler Cash Flow Analysis System), and a computerized system called Project Power Up to begin the management of the business. All this is in exchange for a fee based on sales by its franchisees. As an additional source of income, Cendant also charges reservation and marketing fees. The marketing fee can be calculated as part of the yearly fee or it can be charged separately, in which case it is known as an independent marketing fee.

Cendant Corporation's franchise contracts usually offer the same services, with small variations according to the profile of the franchisee, so that a differentiated product is offered. This shows that the company uses its know-how and infrastructure to achieve a higher market share.

The following shows the company's growth strategy for 2002 in terms of hotel numbers.

Total Hotels	Franchised Hotels	% Franchised Hotels
6,624	6,624	100

Europeans are often surprised that Cendant Corporation does not own a single hotel. Its entire business is based on a franchise system, meaning that the hotel owners assume the biggest risk.[7]

Cendant Corporation's international growth strategy is based on finding new partners willing to subscribe to a master franchise contract. Its European plans consist of developing a minimum of fifty hotels through 2006 under the following agreements:

- Premier Hotels,[8] a British company, signed an agreement with Cendant Corporation in April 1998 to run the Days Inns and Howard Johnson brand names.
- Based in Prague, Keys Inns will be responsible for developing Days Inns in Austria, Bulgaria, Croatia, the Czech Republic, Hungary, Poland, Russia, Slovakia, Slovenia, and the Ukraine.
- A new Cyprus-based company will be responsible for developing the Howard Johnson brand name in Romania.

As of December 31, 2004, Cendant had twenty hotels.

In 2000, Days Inn executives subscribed to seven master franchise contracts in Italy, Jordan, Korea, Taiwan, Morocco, Egypt, and the Dominican Republic. In February 2001, they signed a master franchise contract with Global V Hospitality to develop the brand name in Egypt. The management team hoped to run ten hotels there by 2002, but it did not happen.

Executives of the Days Inn brand name hope to obtain two master franchises per year. At present they are involved in eighteen franchise contracts of this type to develop hotels under this brand name in twenty-nine countries, including Argentina, Bulgaria, Croatia, Egypt, Italy, Japan, Korea, Morocco, Namibia, Paraguay, Poland, Russia, Slovakia, Slovenia, Taiwan, Venezuela, and Zimbabwe. They have expanded heavily into Canada, the Philippines, India, and Mexico. Their plans to increase the Days Inn presence in the United Kingdom, Russia, and eight Eastern European countries by 2004 was more optimistic, as only three of these countries currently have Days Inn hotels.[9]

Choice Hotels International

Choice Hotels International is the world's second biggest hotel franchiser after Cendant Corporation, with eight hotel brand names, three of which are limited to North America.

In 1997 Choice Hotels International became a hotel franchising chain after abandoning its real estate business, which went on to be managed by Sunburst Hospitality Corporation, also a listed company. When the two companies separated, Sunburst Hospitality Corporation owned seventy-five hotels (all in the United States) and 11,000 rooms, as well as twenty hotels that were just about to be inaugurated.

The following shows the company's growth strategy, in terms of hotels, for the year 2002.

Total Hotels	Franchised Hotels	%Franchised Hotels
4,545	4,545	100

Obviously, Choice Hotels International is a pure franchising company, meaning that its owners do not invest in buying hotels, because their entire portfolio consists of franchise contracts.

One of Choice Hotels International's main goals is to expand its franchise system in certain strategic markets. On one hand, the company is making a further incursion into the American market. For this reason, its franchise contracts are currently organized in such a way that they cover five different regions in the United States: the Pacific, the southern Central, the northern Central, the Southeast, and the Northeast. On the other hand, outside the United States, Choice Hotels International is developing a master franchising strategy. Its involvement in this type of company varies a great deal, ranging from no shares at all to 100 percent of the shareholding, depending on the local situation. Some of these franchise contracts cover more than one country.[10]

Choice Hotels International offers its franchisees systems of finance, in collaboration with other financial entities, so that franchisees can develop, purchase, or renovate hotels. The North American hotel chain also offers training services to franchisees and to its own staff at the company's Silver Spring training center. The center runs a course called "Total Lodging by Choice," which is compulsory for all franchisees and is directed at owners and executive directors. Other courses include intensive marketing, booking system, human resources, public relations, and financial management courses.

Choice Hotels International's hotel management system, Profit Manager,[11] is designed to help franchisees achieve optimum profit levels and compete more effectively. Since 1999, Profit Manager has been introduced in 884 U.S. and Canadian hotels. To help launch the system, the company has developed a Technological Support Program (TSP)[12] that allows hotels to pay for Profit Manager (e.g., its software, hardware, maintenance, training, and support) via a leasing system.

The company also has an online management system for purchases: www.ChoiceCentral.com.[13] Thanks to this system, franchisees no longer need to engage in a constant search for suppliers and lower costs, because it allows them to check product specifications, compare products, and obtain supplies at much lower costs, due to commercial agreements with suppliers.

Under the terms of the company's franchise contracts, franchisees have nonexclusive rights to use Choice Hotels International's franchise system in a specific location for a single hotel, normally for a period of twenty years.[14]

When Choice Hotels International sells regional development rights to a master franchisee, the latter becomes responsible for offering Choice Hotels International brand names to local franchisees. The franchisee must also manage all the necessary services (i.e., quality control, bookings, and marketing services) provided as backup for the franchisee hotels in the area covered by the master franchise contract,[15] as well as collect all fees paid by the local franchisees and forward the agreed percentage to Choice Hotels International.

Either of the two parties subscribing to a master franchise contract can terminate the agreement before it expires, providing that certain circumstances occur, such as the master franchisee's inability to make the hotel operators comply with contractual quality control standards. Master franchise agreements normally include clauses that allow the company to terminate the contract if a specific number of hotels are not developed within an established period of time.

Table 9.2 shows the fees that franchisees are charged by some of the hotel chain's brand names. The franchise fees charged by brand names belonging to Choice Hotels International vary. As part of their yearly fee, franchisees make monthly payments to Choice Hotels International that range between 3.5 percent and 5.25 percent of their room revenue. They pay between 1 percent and 3.5 percent as a marketing fee, and between 1.25 percent and 1.75 percent as a booking fee. The initial fee fluctuates between 250 and 300 dollars per hotel room or suite, with a minimum fee ranging between 25,000 and 50,000 dollars according to the brand name under which the hotel operates.

TABLE 9.2. Franchise Fees Charged by Brand Names Belonging to Choice Hotels International, 2002

Brand Name	Initial Fee per Room/Minimum	Royalty Fees (%)	Marketing Fees (%)	Reservation Fees (%)
Comfort Inn	$300/$50,000	5.25	2.1	1.75
Comfort Suites	$300/$50,000	5.25	2.1	1.75
Quality Inn	$300/$35,000	4	2.1	1.75
Quality Suites	$300/$50,000	4	2.1	1.25
Sleep Inn	$300/$40,000	4.5	2.1	1.75
Clarion	$300/$40,000	3.75	1	1.25
Econo Lodge	$250/$25,000	4	3.5[a]	–
Mainstay Suites	$300/$30,000	4.5	2.5[a]	–
Rodeway	$250/$25,000	3.5	1.25	1.25

Source: Annual Report of Choice Hotels International (2002). Available at: phx.corporate-ir.net/phoenix.zhtml?C/99348&p=irol-see.

[a]Including marketing and reservation fees.

Six Continents PLC

Eighty-five percent of Six Continents PLC's hotel portfolio consisted of hotels run under franchise contracts. Six Continents, like other international hotel chains, used the master franchising formula as a means of international growth, as the agreement with the Hoteles Presidente hotel chain shows, aimed at extending the Crowne Plaza brand name throughout Mexico. As a consequence, all the Mexican hotels covered by the agreement were to be transferred to the Crowne Plaza brand name. The objective was for Crowne Plaza to expand its coverage of Mexico's holiday and inner-city hotel markets.

Table 9.3 shows the fees that some of the hotel chain's brand names charge its franchisees. As the table shows, Six Continents PLC's franchise contracts charged an initial fee of 500 dollars per room, with a minimum fee of 40,000 dollars regardless of the brand name in question. Yearly fees ranged from 4.5 percent to 6 percent of the room revenue, while service fees oscillated between 2.5 percent and 3 percent of the room revenue, depending on the brand name.

Hilton Hotels Corporation

Table 9.4 shows franchised hotels under brand names belonging to Hilton Hotels Corporation. The Hampton and Hilton Hotels brand

TABLE 9.3. Franchise Fees Charged by Brand Names Belonging to Six Continents PLC, 2002

Brand Name	Initial Fee	Yearly Fee	Service Fee
Holiday Inn, Holiday Inn Hotels and Suites, Holiday Inn Select	$500 per room, with a $40,000 minimum fee	4.5-6% of the gross revenue per room	2.5% of the gross revenue per room
Holiday Inn Sunspree	$500 per room, with a $40,000 minimum fee	4.5-6% of the gross revenue per room	3% of the gross revenue per room
Holiday Inn Express	$500 per room, with a $40,000 minimum fee	5% of the gross revenue per room	3% of the gross revenue per room
Staybridge Suites	$500 per room, with a $40,000 minimum fee	5% of the gross revenue per room	2.5% of the gross revenue per room

Source: www.intercontinental.com.

TABLE 9.4. Franchised Hotels and Rooms Under Brand Names Belonging to Hilton Hotels Corporation, 2002

Brand Names	Franchised Hotels	Franchised Rooms
Hilton Hotels	170	45,160
Hilton Garden Inn Hotels	84	12,133
Doubletree	48	10,933
Homewood Suites by Hilton	63	6,759
Embassy Suites	73	16,773
Hampton	1,042	107,245
Other brand names	10	1,714

Source: www.hilton.com.

names account for three quarters of the company's franchised rooms. Table 9.5 indicates the fees that some of the hotel chain's brand names charge its franchisees. Hilton Hotels Corporation's franchise contracts charge an initial fee of between 250 and 500 dollars per room, according to the brand name in question. Yearly fees fluctuate between 4 and 5 percent of the room revenue, except for Homewood Suites, which offers discounts during the first two years of business, while service fees stand at 4 percent for all the brand names.

Accor

Table 9.6 shows franchised hotels operating under some of Accor's brand names. The Mercure, Ibis, and Red Roof Inn brand names account for 68 percent of the company's franchised rooms.

SUMMARY

Franchising is a form of cooperation between companies in which one company, the franchiser, grants other companies, the franchisees, the right to commercialize certain types of products and/or services in exchange for some kind of financial compensation. In this chapter, we looked at the whole issue of franchise contracts, from product fran-

TABLE 9.5. Franchise Fees Charged by Some Brand Names Belonging to Hilton Hotels Corporation

Brand Name	Initial Fee	Yearly Fee	Service Fee
Doubletree Hotels	$50,000 for the first 250 rooms, and $250 per additional room	4% of the gross revenue per room	4% of the gross revenue per room
Homewood Suites	$450 per suite, and a $45,000 minimum fee.	4% of the gross revenue per suite	4% of the gross revenue per suite
Embassy Suites	$500 per suite, and a $100,000 minimum fee	5% of the gross revenue per suite	4% of the gross revenue per suite
Hampton Inn & Suites	$450 per room, and a $45,000 minimum fee	5% of the gross revenue per room	4% of the gross revenue per room

Source: www.hilton.com.

TABLE 9.6. Franchised Hotels and Rooms Under Brand Names Belonging to Accor, 2002

Brand Names	Franchised Hotels	Franchised Rooms
Etap	45	3,356
Formule 1	7	464
Ibis	164	11,859
Mercure	156	12,142
Motel 6	86	5,489
Red Roof Inns	72	7,421
Novotel	31	3,804
Sofitel	6	1,214
Otras Marcas	1	325

Source: www.accor.com.

chising to master franchising, and the advantages they entail for the franchiser and the franchisee. The typical fee system for a hotel franchise contract includes an initial fee, yearly fees, marketing fees, and reservation fees. The chapter ended by analyzing how the world's

Top 10 hotel franchisers have used franchises, looking particularly at the cases of Cendant Corporation and Choice Hotels International: companies who run all their hotels under this form of contract. The chapter also contained a breakdown of the franchising fees earned by the hotel chains Choice Hotels International, Six Continents PLC, Hilton Hotels Corporation, and Accor for each of their brand names.

Chapter 10

Management Contracts

THE THEORY

The practice of using business management contracts dates back to the time of the British colonies. The concept was later developed in the United States and then exported to the rest of the world. This type of contract emerged due to an absence of professional training in many sectors. The hotel industry is where management contracts are most widely used.

A business management contract can be defined as a contract under the terms of which a company agrees to manage another one, on behalf of and at the risk of the latter, in exchange for financial remuneration (Sharma, 1984). The application of business management contracts to the hotel sector led to a version known as a hotel management contract (Pérez Moriones, 1998).

Another similar definition with a greater focus on the hotel industry is given by other authors: a management contract is basically an agreement between a hotel management company and the company owning the hotel, under the terms of which the management company runs the hotel.[1] The owner does not make any operational decisions but is responsible for supplying the necessary capital and for meeting the payment of expenses and debts. The management company receives a fee for its services and the owner normally receives the remaining profits after all costs have been deducted.

Management contracts have become a very common feature of hotel operations, taking over from leasing agreements. InterContinental Hotels, which was set up in 1946 as a subsidiary of Pan American World Airways, began to run some of its Latin American hotels under management contracts in the 1950s. Most of Hilton's initial properties were run under a modified leasing agreement, which in some aspects is comparable to today's management contract.

In the United States, management contracts came to the forefront in the 1970s, with Hyatt in the vanguard. This occurred because the increasing price of land, construction costs, and mortgage interest rates made investing in large properties impossible, while the business risks also increased. Thanks to management contracts, the investment risk was transferred from the company running the hotel to the owner. This type of contract also allows hotel chains to expand, achieving greater economies of scale, thus improving the earnings per share (EPS). At the same time, developers without any experience in hotel management were building big 200- or over 300-room hotels, with no desire to run them or an inability to run them at a profit. They therefore turned to hotel organizations with proven ability in the field of management. Meanwhile, some hotel chains that owned their own hotels decided that, due to rising costs, it would be better to get rid of their properties and concentrate on the operational side.[2]

Institutional investors now have accepted the fact that management skills or a capacity for management are the main ingredients needed for successful hotel operations. The investors are prepared to invest millions of dollars in hotel ownership, while the company running the hotels does not need to make a financial commitment. Under the terms of certain management contracts, the operator must invest a small amount of financial capital in the project.

Very often, when a new hotel is built (and also prior to its construction), an agreement is made for a management contract. This enables the company running the hotel to give advice and consultancy on important factors such as the location, financing, and design of the hotel, the negotiation of licenses to open shops in the building, the organization of activities prior to its inauguration, and the selection, hiring, and training of staff.

Generally speaking these contracts are for large-scale projects because hotel chains have more specialist management and supervisory skills in this area. Many new independent companies have also been formed without the high overhead costs of a head office and with a high degree of operational flexibility.[3] These smaller companies often have a short-term management contract from one to ten years and, on occasions, they even take control of properties confiscated by an institutional investor such as a bank until the business recovers and becomes financially viable again. However, management contracts for most hotels are long term, covering periods of up to twenty-five or thirty years. These are sufficiently long periods to cover the length of the loan taken out by the developer.

Some hotel companies operating under franchise contracts offer their management services to franchisees that no longer wish to continue running their hotels themselves. In such cases, the owners must be careful not to take on a long-term management contract that prevents them from selling the properties if they want to, and a cancellation option must be written into the contract to avoid such eventualities.

The hotel chain acting as manager makes the decisions, but the owner incurs the business risks and liabilities. When management contracts were first being used, the owner's responsibility was to provide the items on the inventory and the working capital. The owner also needed to continue injecting capital into the business if losses occurred when things went wrong. This was completely one-sided, benefiting only the management company. The management company's business profits were implicitly guaranteed via a fixed basic fee that was paid regardless of the real profits, meaning that the management company leaders did not need to concern themselves much with controlling costs.[4]

However, as it is becoming more usual for big hotel chains to offer their services through management contracts, competition between hotel chains means that owners/developers can be more selective and demand that the operational and financial liabilities are more equally shared. Indeed they can even demand that the management company contributes a certain amount of capital.

This capital can take several forms: the management company can be asked to pay the preopening costs and/or the initial working capital required, or this sum of money can be extended to include the purchase of furnishings, complementary items, and/or equipment. Some financial contributions to the business can involve a strategic alliance between the owner and the management company, in the sense that both provide a certain amount of cash and sign a joint mortgage on the property.[5]

Management contracts must be designed to suit each individual situation, with special attention to the agreement of fees. The contract must cover matters such as the provision of capital by the management company, if appropriate, the budget and expense limits, accountancy and financial conditions, the length of the contract, a possible renewal clause, the conditions for the cancellation of the contract, services to be provided by the management company, and the minimum annual amount to be spent on advertising, maintenance, replacing furnishings, equipment, and other related items. The contracts should clearly state that this is an agreement between an owner and a hired manager, not a leasing contract. The owner supplies the hotel (i.e., the building, furnishings, decor, equipment, and working capital) and is financially and legally liable for the business. The management company agrees to run the hotel, paying all the expenses on behalf of the owner, and with the earnings it makes, it retains its commission and hands the surplus over to the owner.

The next section outlines the advantages and disadvantages of a management contract for both the management company and the owner of the hotel.

Advantages and Disadvantages for the Management Company

Advantages

- *The financing of the property.* A clear, immediate advantage is the full financing of the business. Unless the owner demands some capital investment, the management company needs little or no initial capital.
- *The reduced risk.* The risks for the company running the hotel deriving from excess building costs, the building process itself, market recessions, or changing markets are all considerably reduced.[6]
- *High ROIs and ROEs.* Indeed, due to the low amount or lack of investment required from the management company, very high financial and economic earnings can be obtained.

Disadvantages

- *Obtaining only part of the profits.* Logically, the other part of the profits are kept by the owner.

- *The loss of the property's potential appreciation.* If a business operation with a management contract is successful, the value of the company will increase. The property owner, not the management company, benefits from this appreciation in value. However, if the value of the property depreciates, as occurred in Asia during the 1998 property crisis, the owner is affected.
- *Obstruction by the owner.* The owner might wish to interfere in the hotel's management tasks, limiting the management company's operational potential.
- *The loss of the contract.* If the management company employees fail to achieve the profit levels that the owner wishes, the contract may be canceled or the company may be sued.
- In time the management contract leads to a *greater diffusion of know-how* than direct investment and thus to a loss of competitive advantages.[7]

Advantages and Disadvantages for the Owner

Advantages

- The risk involved in developing a business activity is reduced.
- A minimum profit is guaranteed and the capital invested will be paid back quickly.
- With the recognition and assimilation of a specific brand name, the value of the company will increase.

Disadvantages

- The operational control over the hotel is lost.
- The management company may not have the necessary resources or experience to adapt to the local culture where the hotel is located.

Fees

Management contracts have three general types of fees: a single basic fee, a basic fee plus an incentive fee, and a basic fee or incentive fee, depending on which is greater.

The Basic Fee System

Under the terms of this agreement, the hotel company receives only a basic fee, which might be up to 5 percent of the hotel's gross earnings. In both America and Europe this 5 percent fee has decreased considerably over time. Alternatively, the basic fee can be based on two separate percentages: one related to the gross room revenue and the other to the gross earnings made from the sale of food and beverages. The basic fee offers no incentive to keep costs down. It encourages maximum sales efforts at the expense of somewhat uncontrolled costs. The owner might well end up with no profits. An incentive fee often is added to encourage the management company to keep costs under control.

The Basic Fee Plus Incentive Fee System

With this system, the basic fee might be a percentage of the gross earnings (normally less than 5 percent) plus an incentive fee of up to 10 percent of the gross operating profit (GOP),[8] i.e., the gross profits earned from running the hotel. Many new variations of this form of payment are feasible, such as those that award a higher incentive fee for a higher GOP. A second alternative is to charge a basic fee that consists partly of a percentage of the room revenue and partly of a percentage of the earnings made from the sale of food and beverages, plus an incentive fee that represents a percentage of the gross profits received from running the hotel. A third alternative is a basic fee based on a fixed sum per available accommodation unit, plus a percentage of the gross profits as an incentive fee. Another variation is to base the incentive fee on the hotel's cash flow.

The Basic Fee or Incentive Fee System

This third type of agreement consists of having either a basic fee or an incentive fee, depending on which is the greatest. Obviously a wide range of alternatives can be possible within this type of system.

EXAMPLES

Table 10.1 shows the world's Top 10 hotel management companies as of 2002. The Top 10 hotel management companies together managed 3,640 hotels or, in other words, 25 percent of their worldwide portfolio. The chains that concentrated most heavily on the management contract strategy did not grow as much as pure franchiser chains.

A direct proportional relation exists between management contracts and a hotel chain's expansion. Five hotel chains from the ranks of the Top 10 hotel management companies (Marriott International, Accor, Six Continents Hotels, Hilton Hotels Corporation, and Starwood Hotels & Resorts Worldwide) belonged to the prestigious club of the ten biggest hotel chains in terms of rooms.

Three companies from the table (Extended Stay America, Tharaldson Enterprises, and Westmont Hospitality Group) are pure management companies, meaning that their entire portfolio is run under management contracts.

As is also the case with franchise contracts, U.S. chains are the maximum exponents of the management contract system. Conse-

TABLE 10.1. Companies That Manage the Most Hotels, 2002

Company	Total Hotels	Hotels Managed	
		Number	Percentage
Marriott International	2,398	798	33
Accor	3,654	511	14
Extended Stay America	431	431	100
Tharaldson Enterprises	341	341	100
Société du Louvre	933	327	35
Six Continents Hotels	3,274	314	10
Westmont Hospitality Group	287	287	100
Starwood Hotels & Resorts Worldwide	743	222	30
Hilton Hotels Corporation	1,986	210	11
Prime Hospitality Group	234	199	85

Source: www.hostelmag.com.

quently, owners of European and Asian chains should take good note of this, increasing their involvement in contracts of this type, because, with virtually the same amount of investment as that needed for a franchise, much higher profit levels can be obtained.

As also happens with franchise contracts, management contracts involve lower investment risks and a reduced cyclical risk for the business when compared with the ownership of a hotel.

Regarding the fees involved, strong promotion of the incentive fee and a big reduction in the basic fee are likely, leading in some cases to its total disappearance.

Marriott International

Marriott International is the world's leading hotel management chain, and it manages 974 hotels.

Marriott International's rapid expansion began in 1995, when owners acquired 49 percent of the shares of the luxury Ritz Carlton Hotel Company. In late 1996, they offered 1 billion dollars, a sum higher than that offered by Doubletree Hotels, to buy the Renaissance Hotels Group.[9] This purchase virtually doubled Marriott International's capacity outside the United States, combining the company's 10,000 rooms in its fifty hotels outside the United States with the 46,500 rooms belonging to the Renaissance Group's 150 hotels, most of which were also located outside the United States. Marriott International's resulting portfolio includes strong brand names covering a wide range of different market segments, with just a few anomalies still to be resolved. It is also expanding its European operations with the purchase of the hotel groups Swallow in the United Kingdom and Treff in Germany.

Marriott International's ten brand names covered all segments of the market. It was positioned in the reasonably priced segment with its Fairfield and TownePlace Suites brand names. In the midrange segment, it had the following three brand names: Courtyard, Residence Inn, and Ramada. It was positioned at the top end of the market with the following four brand names: Marriott, New World, Renaissance, and J.W. Marriott. Finally, it was also present in the luxury segment with the Ritz-Carlton brand name.

Marriott International is present in sixty countries. The main ones are the United States, with 80 percent of the company's rooms, the United Kingdom, with 3 percent, and China and Canada, each with 2 percent of its rooms.

This American multinational is much more familiar with client satisfaction than many other hotel chains because, as a high percentage of its portfolio is run under management contracts, it is in more direct contact with clients than companies operating through a franchise contract. Nevertheless, its growth is limited by the need to engage qualified staff.[10]

Accor

As of December 31, 2002, Accor runs more than 500 hotels under management contracts. The French multinational is a company with numerous different types of businesses and many different travel and leisure activities. In addition to hotels, its best-known company is the travel agency, Carlson Wagonlit Travel, in which it has a 50 percent stake together with Carlson Hospitality Worldwide. Approximately 17 percent of the company is in the hands of major shareholders, including its founders Paúl Dubrule and Gérard Pélisson. The company is listed on the Paris stock exchange, France, where its head office is situated.

Accor is present in 140 countries. The foremost ones are the United States, with 33 percent of the group's rooms; France with 28 percent; Germany with almost 8 percent; and Australia with 4 percent of the company's rooms.

Table 10.2 shows Accor's management-contract portfolio broken down into brand names. The Mercure, Novotel, and Sofitel brand names account for 84 percent of all the French group's rooms that are run under managment contract.

Extended Stay America

As already mentioned, Extended Stay America is a pure management chain. The American company has focused its efforts on long-stay hotels for business and leisure travelers. At present its expansion is limited to the states, although this is no impediment to the com-

TABLE 10.2. Hotels and Rooms Under Management Contract Belonging to Accor Brand Names, 2002

Accor's Brand Names	Hotels Under Management Contract	Rooms Under Management Contract
Etap	5	326
Formule 1	5	436
Ibis	54	6,792
Mercure	194	20,124
Motel 6	2	117
Red Roof Inns	–	–
Novotel	97	18,074
Sofitel	77	13,602
Other brand names	22	2,476

Source: www.accor.com.

pany's rapid growth. Extended Stay America is listed on the American stock exchange, the country where it also has its head office.

Through its four brand names, Extended Stay America and Homestead Studio Suites operate in three of the market's four segments; it is not represented in the midrange segment. It is positioned at the cheaper end of the market with its Crossland Economy Studios brand name. Meanwhile, at the top end of the market, it is represented by Extended Stay America Efficiency Studios, and it is positioned in the luxury segment with the StudioPLUS Deluxe Studios brand name.

Tharaldson Enterprises

Like Extended Stay America, Tharaldson Enterprises is also a pure management company. The hotel chain specializes in the development and management of motels, run under several different brand names such as Days Inn or Homewood Suites. The company's success has also been shared by its employees, who own half the company's shares, while the other half is held by its founder, Gary Tharaldson. This hotel chain is not a listed company. Its head office is in the United States, where all its hotels are located.

Tharaldson Enterprises operates at the cheaper end of the market through the following brand names: Residence Inn by Marriott, SpringHill Suites, TownePlace Suites, Fairfield Inn, Express by Holiday Inn, Country Inns & Suites, Homewood Suites, Hampton Inn & Suites, Hampton Inn, Hawthorn Suites, AmericInn, Days Inn, Super 8 Motel, MainStay Suites, Quality Suites, Comfort Suites, Comfort Inn, Sleep Inn, and Econo Lodge.

Société du Louvre

Société du Louvre, which runs over one-third of its portfolio under management contracts, owns two hotel groups: Concorde and the Envergure Group. Since its acquisition of the Hotels & Compagnie Group in June 1999, Envergure has added the Climat de France, Nuit d'Hotel, and Balladins brand names to its portfolio and, in 2000, it created a new brand name, Kyriad. The company is listed on the stock exchange in France, where its head office is located. Its principal shareholder is the Taittinger family. Modifications took place in the company's modes of management and administration. The company became a public limited company with a board of directors as of January 14, 2003.

Société du Louvre is present in twenty-two countries, although it operates mainly in France, where 90 percent of the company's rooms are found. The remaining 10 percent are located primarily in Belgium, Luxembourg, and Switzerland.

Six Continents Hotels

Six Continents Hotels ran 10 percent of its portfolio, or 314 of its hotels, under management contracts. In 1998, Six Continents (formerly known as Bass Hotels & Resorts) underwent significant modifications as a result of two changes. First, by taking over InterContinental Hotels, the group's leaders found the company strongly positioned at the top end of the market and also able to break away from Holiday Inn brand-name derivatives. Second, an agreement with Bristol Hotels gave the company a new corporate structure, allowing it to compete with "new" rapid-growth hotel companies. The company was listed on the United Kingdom stock market, although its hotel division's head office was in the United States.

In 2000, with the sale of the Bass Brewers division, the company leaders centered their efforts on the hotel business. During the same year, the takeovers of Bristol Hotels and SPHC confirmed Six Continents PLC's commitment to continue its growth and its goal to become the world's leading hotel company. Six Continents Hotels' possible interest in the portfolio of the Granada Compass chain once again put the company in the spotlight.

Six Continents Hotels was present in 100 countries. The main ones were the United States (with 65 percent of the company's rooms), Germany and the United Kingdom (each with 3 percent of its rooms), and Mexico and China (each with 2 percent of the company's rooms).

Westmont Hospitality Group

Westmont Hospitality Group, as with Extended Stay America and Tharaldson Enterprises, is a pure management chain. The American company is not listed on the stock market and is owned by the Mangalji family. Its corporate office is in the United States.

Westmont operates in different segments of the market through the following brand names: Holiday Inn, Crowne Plaza, Radisson, Sheraton, Doubletree, Embassy Suites, and Delta.

Westmont Hospitality is present in eight countries. Its primary presence is in the United States, with 65 percent of the company's rooms, with other hotels in Germany, Belgium, France, the United Kingdom, Spain, Italy, and Canada.

Starwood Hotels & Resorts Worldwide

Starwood Hotels & Resorts Worldwide ran 222 hotels under management contracts, representing 30 percent of its portfolio. During the past few years, the company has increased the number of management contracts it holds considerably, and this accounts for a large part of the group's growth. At the same time, it has reduced its other contracts (i.e., franchises) and its ownership of property and leaseholds.[11]

The company, which is a relatively new arrival to the international hotel industry, began as two companies: Starwood Hotels & Resorts, a real estate investment company (an REIT), and Starwood Hotels & Resorts Worldwide, a company dedicated to the management and running of hotels. In 1998, due to a change in U.S. tax legislation, the two companies were forced to merge, forming Starwood Hotels & Resorts Worldwide, Inc., with a main office in Maryland. Its subsidiary, Starwood Hotels & Resorts, is a real estate investment company, also based in Maryland. The company is listed on the U.S. stock market.

The group's leaders made two significant attempts at expansion in 1998 by taking over Westin Hotels and ITT Corporation (the owner of Sheraton Hotels), thereby changing a small hotel group into one of the world hotel industry's giants. Starwood Hotels & Resorts Worldwide, with its Sheraton and Westin brand names, is clearly a leader in the top segment of the market.

Starwood Hotels & Resorts Worldwide is present in eighty-two countries, mainly the United States (with 58 percent of the company's rooms), Canada (with 7 percent), and Germany (with 3 percent of its rooms).

Given the diverse portfolios of the groups taken over by Starwood Hotels & Resorts Worldwide, the company is involved in different types of operations. For example, its Sheraton[12] operations include hotels that it owns as well as management and franchise contracts. In contrast, Westin, an international management company, has generally followed the same growth strategy since its foundation, i.e., management contracts.[13]

Within this category of hotel belonging to Starwood Hotels & Resorts Worldwide's European subsidiary are hotels located in unique buildings in cities such as Milan, Rome, Vienna, and Madrid.[14]

Hilton Hotels Corporation

Hilton Hotels Corporation, a California-based firm that has been listed on the New York stock market since 1946, is the hotel chain with the world's most valuable brand names. It is a pure hotel company, as its gaming division separated from the company in 1998. The American chain's future strategy depends on its alliance with Hilton International and on its acquisition of the hotel chain Promus.

In 2002, Hilton Hotels Corporation had an 8 percent degree of internationalization, with seventy-nine hotels and almost 25,000 rooms in international markets. Its greatest expansion has taken place in North America, more specifically in Canada and Mexico, with a total of thirty and twelve hotels, respectively. It has a low degree of inter-nationalization due to the fact that Hilton International held the rights to the Hilton brand name outside North America.

Executives of the Hilton Hotels Corporation, a company that emerged during the 1950s with the acquisition and subsequent resto-ration of old hotels such as the Stevens in Chicago and the Plaza in New York, fell into debt and experienced firsthand the risks of being hotel owners. That was why, when they developed the first of their Caribbean hotels (under the name "Caribe Hilton" in San Juan, Puerto Rico), they did so under a leasing contract with the govern-ment equivalent to two-thirds of the gross earnings. Thus Hilton Ho-tels Corporation became a pioneer in the development of growth strategies based on leasing contracts. All the company needed to sup-ply in exchange were the total opening costs and those funds needed to start the business. This served as a precedent for later hotels in places such as Istanbul, Mexico, and Cuba. In Cuba the company experienced losses as a result of the political instability (with occu-pancy figures of 14 percent). As a result, the company was forced to hand the hotel over to Cuba's government.

This was probably the main reason why the company started to convert all its leasing contracts into management contracts. In both cases, the hotel chain had control over the running of the hotel. Hilton Hotels Corporation, a pioneer in contracts of this kind, introduced the fee system via the application of a basic 5 percent fee and an incentive fee equivalent to 10 percent of the GOP.

Table 10.3 shows Hilton Hotels Corporation's portfolio of hotels run under management contracts as of 2002, broken down into differ-ent brand names. The Doubletree, Homewood Suites by Hilton, and Hilton Hotels brand names make up 82 percent of the company's rooms run under management contracts.

Prime Hospitality

Prime Hospitality could be regarded as a pure hotel management company, as it manages 85 percent of its portfolio (equivalent to al-most 200 hotels). The company is listed on the U.S. stock market, where its head office is situated as well as its entire portfolio.

TABLE 10.3. Hotels and Rooms Under Management Contract Belonging to Hilton Hotels Corporation's Different Brand Names, 2002

Hilton Hotels Corporation's Brand Names	Hotels Under Management Contract	Rooms Under Management Contract
Hilton Hotels	14	10,207
Hilton Garden Inn Hotels	–	–
Doubletree	62	17,295
Homewood Suites by Hilton	24	2,820
Embassy Suites	57	14,375
Hampton	12	1,603
Other brand names	22	4,822

Source: www.hilton.com.

Prime Hospitality operates its Wellesley Inns & Suites brand name in the midrange segment of the market and AmeriSuites at the top end of the market. The company also has franchise contracts for brand names operating in the same segment of the market, such as Hilton, Radisson, and Crowne Plaza, together with midrange brand names such as Days Inn, Howard Johnson, Comfort Inn & Suites, and Ramada.

Sol Meliá

Some executives of European hotel chains such as Sol Meliá are beginning to realize how profitable management contracts can be. Initially the owners of the Majorcan chain owned most of their hotels. Now they focus strongly on management contracts; this is currently their main growth strategy, accounting for 48 percent of the company's portfolio.[15]

Between 1993 and 1996, coinciding with a general crisis in the tourist industry, Sol Meliá expanded most heavily into management and franchise contracts. In 1996, the group separated its hotel ownership business (based around Hoteles Meliá, which later changed its name to Inmotel Inversiones) from its management and franchise operations (centered on Sol Meliá). In July of the same year, Sol Meliá was launched on the Madrid stock exchange.

In 1996 all the revenue from the company's stock market launch was invested in Inmotel Inversiones. With these funds, a large part of Inmotel Inversiones' outstanding debt was written off, allowing the group to rectify its financial situation completely, renovate hotels, and also continue its expansion by acquiring new ones. Since then Inmotel executives have focused their energies on real estate management.

Since 1997, the Majorcan chain has focused its activities on management contracts, gradually incorporating new Spanish and international hotels. In the same year, Sol Meliá and Inmotel formed Meliá Inversiones Americanas (MIA) to speed up the chain's Latin American growth, a priority area for the group's expansion strategy. Given MIA's lack of stock market success, Sol Meliá made a takeover bid for MIA's entire share capital, leading to a final shareholding of 97.12 percent.

The earnings from Sol Meliá's management contracts are shown in Table 10.4. The basic fee represents 63 percent of the management contract's total fee (i.e., the basic fee plus the incentive fee). In other words, it is 63 percent of the hotel's total sales. The incentive fee, which is a percentage of the GOP, accounts for the remaining 37 percent. Only in the case of the group's American hotels that are run under management contract is the incentive fee higher than the basic fee. Cuba is quite the opposite, as its basic fee is three times higher than its incentive fee. From 1998 to 2000 the total fee grew by 30 percent, due to an increase in the basic fee (29 percent), rather than an increase in the incentive fee (22 percent). Sol Meliá's main markets, in terms of earnings from management contracts, are the European holiday hotel market and Cuba.

SUMMARY

A hotel management contract is an agreement between a hotel management company and a company owning a hotel, under the terms of which the former is commissioned with running the hotel. The owner does not make any operational decisions but is responsible for supplying the necessary capital and for meeting the payment of expenses and debts. The management company receives a fee for its services, and the owner normally receives the remaining profits after

TABLE 10.4. The Earnings from Sol Meliá's Management Contracts

Euros (Millions)	1998	1999	2000
European Holiday Hotels			
Basic fee	5.361	5.223	6.202
Incentive fee	2.158	3.456	4.453
European Inner-City Hotels			
Basic fee	4.916	5.223	5.998
Incentive fee	1.833	1.815	1.947
America			
Basic fee	2.488	3.426	4.027
Incentive fee	3.991	3.330	4.261
Asia & the Pacific			
Basic fee	1.328	1.557	1.881
Incentive fee	1.430	1.436	1.869
Cuba			
Basic fee	5.139	6.443	7.483
Incentive fee	2.506	2.554	2.380
Total basic fee	19.232	21.872	25.591
Total incentive fee	11.918	12.591	14.910
Total fees	31.150	34.463	40.501

Source: www.solmelia.com.

all costs have been deducted. One of the sectors in which management contracts play a key role is the hotel industry. This chapter provided an in-depth analysis of hotel management contracts, including the pros and cons of this strategy for both the owner and the hotel management company. The most typical fee system with a hotel management contract is a combination of a basic fee and an incentive fee. The chapter concluded by looking at how the world's Top 10 hotel management chains have developed this strategy. Marriott International has the world's largest room management portfolio. Other major examples are the pure management chains Extended Stay America, Tharaldson Enterprises, and Westmont Hospitality Group.

Chapter 11

Leaseholds and Ownership

THE THEORY

A leasehold contract can be defined as renting a hotel for a certain period of time, normally never less than three years, and subject to automatic renewal. In the hotel industry, the object of the contract is the business, rather than the hotel and all its belongings, furniture, and fittings. Usually, the leaseholder is a hotel group, so the leasehold tends to involve the hotel's assumption of the corporate image and production process of the hotel chain acting as leaseholder. The lessor tends to be responsible for any annual amortization costs, as well as the maintenance and conservation of the building in optimum conditions.

The financial remuneration paid by the leaseholder to the lessor can take several forms, although the most customary ones are as follows:

- The payment of a fixed yearly fee, which is reviewed annually to comply with a certain stipulation, normally the price index
- The payment of a percentage, often about 5 percent, of the hotel earnings
- The payment of a percentage, often about 15 percent, of the cash flow generated
- Either of the last two systems, plus a fixed sum of money

When stipulated by the lessor, it is customary to agree on the payment by the leaseholder of a fixed yearly sum to cover replacement costs relating to the hotel's different services. For this reason, an inventory is usually taken of all the belongings and facilities that are leased, with a view to settling any future disputes.

The owner of the hotel is entitled to inspect the property to check the conservation of the facilities. Once the contract has come to an end, the hotel chain must return the buildings and the furnishings and fittings to the owner in the same condition as they were in at the beginning of the contract.[1]

In practice, a traditional rental agreement is usually arranged when the leasehold is for a short period of time, for example two or three years. However, when the leasehold is for a longer period of time, such as seven or eight years, a leasing agreement is signed, i.e., a leasehold with purchase rights, instead of a traditional rental agreement.

A hotel chain that has entered into a leasehold agreement may also subscribe to a management contract with another chain, without the consent of the hotel owner if it is thus stipulated in the leasehold contract.

Ownership consists of the total or partial acquisition of a hotel. Its main advantage is that the hotel's total profits are kept by the owner or owners. Nevertheless, given the large amount of finance that this growth strategy requires, it is almost unviable when talking about hotel chains the size of those in the United States, where Cendant Corporation alone has more hotel beds than an entire country with a strong tourist industry, such as Spain.

Consequently, hotel ownership is the slowest, least profitable, and most operationally and financially risky growth strategy of all the different strategies aimed at expansion.

To what extent these two systems have been used by the world's ten hotel chains with the greatest number of rooms is discussed next.

EXAMPLES

Table 11.1 shows the percentage of hotels owned and operated under leasehold contracts by the world's Top 10 hotel chains with the greatest number of rooms. The hotel chains that make up the world's Top 10 chains with the greatest number of rooms either own or lease a total of 2,931 hotels, representing 10 percent of their joint world portfolio. Accor alone accounts for 81 percent of these hotels. Hotel own-

TABLE 11.1. Hotels Owned or Run Under Leasehold Contracts by the World's Top 10 Hotel Chains with the Greatest Number of Rooms, 2002

Hotel Company	Total Hotels	Hotels Owned and Leased	
		Number	Percentage
Cendant Corporation	6,624	–	0
Six Continents Hotels	3,274	191	6
Marriott International	2,398	–	0
Accor	3,654	2,386	65
Choice Hotels International	4,545	–	0
Hilton Hotels Corporation	1,986	71	4
Best Western International	4,052	–	0
Starwood Hotels & Resorts Worldwide	743	165	22
Carlson Hospitality Worldwide	788	–	0
Sol Meliá	350	148	42

ership or leasehold contracts are not priority systems for any of the U.S. hotel chains belonging to the world Top 10.

The European chains have concentrated the most on leasehold contracts and hotel ownership; these systems account for 65 percent of Accor's portfolio and 42 percent of Sol Meliá's. Starwood Hotels & Resorts Worldwide and Hilton Hotels Corporation are the only U.S. chains in the Top 10 that have used both systems, and they account for 22 percent of Starwood's portfolio and just 4 percent of that of Hilton Hotels Corporation.

Cendant Corporation, Marriott International, Choice Hotels International, and Carlson Hospitality Worldwide have not used ownership or leasehold contracts at all.[2]

During periods of financial hardship, such as the period immediately after September 11, 2001, an interesting strategy enables a company to sell a hotel, thus obtaining cash, while continuing to run it under a long-term contract. This is the sale and leaseback system.

With hotel ownership and leasehold contracts, hotel chains have greater control over the quality of the hotel product than with franchises or management contracts. This is why the Spanish chain NH Hoteles has tended to use both the former systems.

SUMMARY

A leasehold contract can be defined as an agreement to rent a hotel for a certain period of time. Usually the leaseholder is a hotel group, so the leasehold tends to involve the lessor's acceptance of its corporate image and production process. The typical fee system with a leasehold contract consists of one of the following: a fixed yearly sum adjusted in accordance with the Consumer Price Index, a percentage of the earnings, a percentage of the cash flow, or either of the last two fees combined with a fixed amount.

Ownership consists of the total or partial acquisition of a hotel. Given the large amount of finance that this growth strategy requires, it is the slowest, least profitable, riskiest growth strategy of all.

The chapter finished by analyzing to what extent leasehold or ownership contracts have been introduced by the world's 10 hotel chains with the largest room portfolios. European chains stand out particularly, since they are the maximum exponents of these systems in contrast with their use of franchise or management contracts.

Chapter 12

Branding

THE THEORY

Branding plays a fundamental role in product strategies. On one hand, to develop a product under a particular brand name requires substantial long-term investment, particularly for publicity and promotion. It would be easier if manufacturers made products so that others could give them a brand name. This is what manufacturers from Taiwan do. They produce a large amount of the clothes, household electronic appliances, and computers that are sold worldwide, but not under Taiwanese brand names. However, these manufacturers also realize that the real power is in the hands of companies with recognized brand names, as they can replace their Taiwan-manufactured products with cheaper ones made in Malaysia or alternative locations.

In contrast, Japanese and South Korean companies avoided this mistake. They invested sufficient amounts of capital to create their own brand names for their products, such as Sony and Toyota. Consequently, when they can no longer cope with production in their own country, their brands will still continue to generate a sense of client loyalty.

A strong brand name has loyal clients; this is evidenced when a sufficient number of consumers request this brand and refuse to buy substitute ones, even at lower prices. Mercedes, for instance, has clients who are faithful to it. Companies developing brand names that generate a high degree of loyalty are, to a certain extent, protected from the effects of the promotional activities of their rivals (Kotler, 1996).

The following terminology is used in branding:

- A *brand:* A name, term, sign, symbol, or design (or a combination of them) used to identify the goods or services of a seller or group of sellers, so as to distinguish them from those of its/their rivals.

- A *brand name:* The part of the brand that can be verbalized, for example, Holiday Inn, Motel 6, or Super 8 Motels.
- The *brand symbol:* The part of the brand that can be recognized but not spoken, such as designs, signs, or distinctive colors. An example is the rounded "H" used by Hilton hotels.
- A *registered trademark:* The brand or part of it that is legally protected and may be appropriated for sole or exclusive use. A registered trademark protects a seller's sole right to use a brand name or its symbols.
- *Copyright:* Sole legal rights to reproduce, publish, and sell the contents and form of literary, musical, or artistic work.

Deciding on a brand name is a challenge for marketing experts. The key decisions involved are shown in Figure 12.1. Customer loyalty in tourism is hard to achieve even when clients are very satisfied with their holiday experience, as their curiosity leads them to be attracted to other alternatives. Tourists are continually looking for new experiences, new places, new airlines, and new accommodations. For all of these reasons, creating a sense of loyalty to a particular brand name is difficult. Therefore *branding* is very important. In addition, the speed with which new brands[1] are launched makes the task of the travel agent a difficult one.

Brands are created to stimulate consumer awareness and to encourage purchases and a sense of loyalty toward the product in question. During the mature stage of its life cycle, the hotel industry needs to develop strong brands in order to survive in such a highly competitive environment.[2]

To maintain client loyalty to a particular brand, the following factors must be taken into account: (1) each brand must be defined so as to conform to certain specifications that must be adapted to the chosen market segment; (2) each brand must be created to conform to consistent quality standards, so as to attract different market segments; (3) each brand's image must be used in a consistent way by all the chain's hotels.

Three reasons explain why hotel chains have developed different brands (Olsen, Damonte, and Jackson, 1989):

1. Executives' desire to have a portfolio with a range of different products, thus enabling the hotel chain to diversify its risk.

2. The proliferation of brands that characterizes the hotel industry can be attributed to the leaders' desires to satisfy their own needs, rather than those of their clients. The move toward segmentation may be motivated by owners of hotel companies and the potential that their franchisees offer (Withiam, 1985). Brands are also created in response to a need to maintain company growth in a saturated market and a need to rationalize or unify a chain that is inconsistent, given the heterogeneity of hotel chains' different hotel properties (Withiam, 1985).

3. It is more cost-effective to create new brands than to renovate existing hotels.

After a market has been segmented into appropriate variables such as descriptive, psychological, psychographic, and behavioral vari-

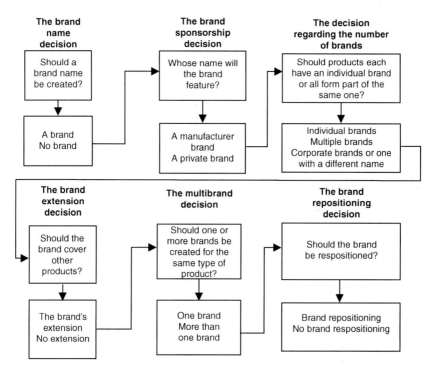

FIGURE 12.1. Brand-Related Decisions (*Source:* Kotler, Philip, *Marketing Management: Analysis, Planning, Implementation, and Control,* 6th Edition, © 1988. Reprinted by permission of Pearson Education, Inc., Upper Saddle River, NJ.)

ables, positioning occurs. This is the process through which a hotel organization tries to notify its target market of features that distinguish its product from those of its rivals (Crawford-Welch, 1991). Many hotel chains have had limited success in positioning multiple brands: the success of a multiple brand depends on the creation and, more important, maintenance of clear differentiation in consumers' minds (Yesawich, 1985).

Brand-related aspects play an increasingly important role in the strategies adopted by hotel companies. Many see their ownership of these brands as a central part of their business plan and try to seek expansion opportunities that can give added value to these brands.

Price Waterhouse Coopers (PWC) has identified five types of brand ownership by hotel companies:

1. *Monolithic.* This is a single-brand approach usually associated with direct ownership or management. An example is the Hilton Group in the United Kingdom, but even in this case the group's brand portfolio is likely to be extended in the near future to allow for expansion through acquisition.
2. *Umbrella.* The brands operated by the company have some generic attributes but cover a range of different segments and operational types. Marriott International is an example of this, with Courtyard by Marriott, core brand Marriott hotels, Fairfield Inn by Marriott, and Residence Inn by Marriott.
3. *Endorsement.* This approach is adopted mostly by consortia such as Best Western. The brand has only limited generic attributes, and it acts as little more than a name above a door, providing marketing and reservation services.
4. *Co-branding.* This has been adopted by weaker national brands to achieve leverage from more widely recognized international brands. Examples include Arabella Sheraton in Germany and Radisson SAS.
5. *Multiple.* This involves a broad grouping together of brands that have few characteristics in common. InterContinental has moved increasingly toward this approach, dropping Holiday Inn from Crowne Plaza and repositioning Express by changing its name from Holiday Inn Express to Express by Holiday Inn. Its Inter-

Continental brand is not associated with Holiday Inn at all. Previously, InterContinental could have been classed as using the umbrella approach.

Advantages and Disadvantages of Branding in the Hotel Industry

Advantages

- Commercial brands make it easier for consumers to identify a product or service, so a customer can request a service by its name.[3] For consumers, a brand must be consistent. Therefore, the brand name must be simple and easy to remember. For instance, Western International Hotels changed its name to Westin Hotels in 1981.
- For customers, a brand ensures the quality of a particular product or service. The Waldorf Astoria in New York is suggestive of a high degree of quality, whereas Comfort Inns suggest more economical prices.
- A brand creates an image not only for the product or service, but also for the company.
- Commercial brands make it simpler for consumers to compare prices. Thus consumers can easily compare different products belonging to closely related brands. For example, Carnival Cruise Lines associates the idea of "fun ships" with its brand, whereas the Queen Elizabeth II's promotional slogan ("For once in your life, live!") implies a unique experience.
- Consumers take a minimum of risks. Therefore, a specific brand's product or service must meet their expectations.
- Different market segments can be attracted by using multiple brands. Managers of chains such as Hilton International and InterContinental (and they were not the only ones) thought that they should focus only on inner-city hotels, centering their operations on business travel (their original market), but then they realized that this kind of customer also takes vacations, and this is how both hotel chains expanded into the vacation hotel market.
- Tourism and the travel industry are highly competitive businesses that are heavily dependent on travel agencies and tour op-

erators. Customers and travel agents can easily remember major brands, and travel agents are quick to recommend leading brands to their customers.

Disadvantages

If all of a chain's hotels belong to the same brand, an image of consistency within the chain's chosen market is ensured. However, difficulties emerge when a standard service is offered at all of the brand's hotels, because the hotel product's standard features can actually be detrimental to a brand's consistency. It is very hard to control certain intangible factors, such as staff behavior or the experience of individual consumers at given moments. Due to this situation, five main problems can arise (Slattery, 1988):

1. Products dependent on the hotel's internal specifications are regularly modernized and replaced with new ones. These internal specifications involve decisions on the type, quality, and style of furnishings and other basic equipment needed to run the hotel, which affect all of the company's departments.
2. Any changes or alterations to these internal specifications are usually carried out as part of specific programs. This means that hotels can appear completely different from one another, as these changes are not introduced simultaneously in all of the chain's hotels.
3. The demand for a specific brand experienced by some hotels will not necessarily be the same as that experienced by other hotels run under the same brand name. The hotel chain leaders may decide to reduce the room rates in those hotels with low occupancy figures.
4. Ensuring hotels' standard external appearance is difficult, due to the strict limitations that countries impose on the construction of new hotels.
5. It is very difficult for international hotel chains to achieve a particular brand image. First, this image can vary from country to country, as is the case of Sofitel, a brand with a luxury image in France and a very different image internationally. This is precisely why the Accor group was interested in buying the Le

Méridien hotel chain: it could be used to replace the Sofitel brand name in international markets. Second, customers may be confused regarding the image of a specific brand, since some hotel chains offer a brand covering different categories of hotel. This is the case of Starwood Hotels & Resorts Worldwide, which operates three-, four-, and five-star hotels under its Westin brand name. The same is also true of Best Western International, which runs a wide range of hotels of different categories, despite its recognition as an operator in the midrange segment of the market. In these cases, the only indicator of the hotel's category is its price.

Hotel chains achieve brand consistency and recognition if they manage to meet, or indeed exceed, their clients' expectations.[4] Hotel chains use multibranding as an alternative way of achieving this consistency, because it enables them to avoid any change in the image of its main brand when focusing on new market segments. This is exactly what Starwood Hotels & Resorts Worldwide has done by introducing the Four Points brand name (directed at the midrange segment of the market), so as not to alter the high-quality image of its Sheraton brand name. Similarly, Six Continents Hotels used the Crowne Plaza brand name to penetrate the top end of the market, instead of doing so with its main Holiday Inn name, as the latter is directed at the midrange segment.

The multibranding strategy does not guarantee success. Indeed, several companies either have or have had too many brand names. An example is Marriott International, which currently needs to restructure its brands following the acquisition of a large number of different ones as a result of its purchase of the Renaissance and Ritz-Carlton groups. Holiday Inn's branding strategy also required substantial restructurization, such as the process underwent by the Accor group, which reduced its brands by 50 percent, from fourteen to just seven. Starwood Hotels & Resorts Worldwide needs to carry out an in-depth review of its branding policy. It has little coverage of the midrange segment of the market, with only 150 or so Four Points hotels, and a lack of clarity in its top-range market policy.

Brands have played a key role in the expansion of multinational hotel chains by offering access to major advantages, including more powerful marketing systems, more effective booking systems, stronger sales networks, and greater purchasing power.

Consultants from Arthur Andersen cite five key reasons why strong brands are on the increase:

1. Normally they obtain higher market shares.
2. Often they obtain price premiums from customers.
3. Typically they achieve higher returns for investors.
4. They offer avenues for potentially diverse means of further growth.
5. They create a sense of customer loyalty and therefore generate more stable earnings streams.

Hotel chain leaders working for prestigious brand names can finance their activities at a lower cost than competitors with weaker brand names. Indeed, this has motivated hotel chains from the first group to make numerous takeover bids for rival firms with less powerful brands.

Big hotel chains can benefit from economies of scale, as well as from being able to invest in key areas such as technology. Small hotel chains or private hotels have difficulty competing with these giants, except when the big chains are positioned in a highly specialized segment such as boutique hotels, in which brands such as Malmaison (owned by Radisson SAS) and the W brand (owned by Starwood Hotels & Resorts Worldwide) operate.

A brand's prestige is a key factor in hotel chain expansion, particularly when franchise and management contracts are involved. Having a prestigious brand makes reaching a franchise or management-contract agreement with hotel owners much easier.

A brand's internationality is crucially important for any hotel company with worldwide pretensions, as it greatly facilitates a chain's expansion into international markets. This accounts for the almost nonexistent internationalization of Cendant Corporation and the scanty internationalization of Choice Hotels International. Despite the fact that they rank first and fifth among the top hotel chains with the greatest number of rooms, they lack strong international brand names.

Hotel chain operators must ensure that their clients are faithful to their brands. Their response to the globalization of the hotel industry is to encourage and consolidate brand loyalty. As a result, a large part of the hotel groups' publicity focuses on forming brand loyalty rather than on promoting a particular hotel in a specific location. As an example, note the slogan used by Hilton Hotels Corporation: "Take me to the Hilton."

International marketing alliances can help to combat a brand's lack of international coverage. One brand alone cannot cover every single city in the world where a hotel market is present. Consequently, brands run the risk of losing client loyalty if a client is occasionally forced to travel to a destination where the brand is not represented.

Branding strategy is crucial for hotel chains' future expansion. In the international hotel trade, the future of a branding strategy is dependent on a number of different concepts. These include differentiation and internationalization.

- *Differentiation.* When positioning a brand, most hotel chains have based their strategy on functional or objective attributes (i.e., the advantages the hotels offer for carrying out business, ease of payment from the hotel room, etc). However, scant attention has been given to emphasizing products' "subjective attributes" (i.e., better service or friendlier staff) as a positioning strategy.
- *Internationalization.* International hotel chain executives must decide whether sufficient similarities between different countries' market segments merit the creation of a brand directed at international markets.

The next section highlights the international hotel trade's most representative brands.

EXAMPLES

Table 12.1 shows the twenty brands with the greatest number of hotel rooms in the world as of 2002.

Best Western International

Best Western International is the only member of the world's Top 10 with a single brand. Best Western International is widely regarded

TABLE 12.1. Twenty Biggest Hotel Brands, 2002

Brand	Rooms
Best Western International	306,851
Holiday Inn	294,493
Days Inn	164,092
Marriott Hotels, Resorts & Suites	158,112
Comfort Inn	131,647
Sheraton Hotels & Resorts	127,904
Super 8 Motels	125,016
Ramada Franchise Systems	120,515
Hampton Inn & Suites	117,806
Express by Holiday Inn	103,522
Radisson Hotels & Resorts	100,874
Motel 6	90,276
Hilton Hotels Corporation	86,063
Quality	84,760
Courtyard by Marriott	78,785
Mercure	72,536
Hilton International	66,245
Hyatt Regency	65,576
Ibis	60,939
Novotel	57,917

Source: www.hostelmag.com.

as a consortium that is positioned in the midrange segment of the market, but this single brand covers a wide variety of different categories of hotel. For example, in the United States Best Western International has two-star hotels as well as more than 100 luxury hotels, in the latter case with room rates of over 200 dollars per night.

Holiday Inn

Holiday Inn (InterContinental's leading brand, which was originally developed in the United States) has hotels in cities, near interstates, and close to airports. Holiday Inns are full-service, midrange hotels, directed at clients traveling with their families or alone, for either business or leisure purposes.

An extensive modernization program is being carried out in the United States to convert these hotels into "the Holiday Inns of the Future." In January 2000, the first of these hotels was opened in Atlanta. They will act as a prototype for a new generation of hotels, which will be distinguishable from the rest due to the new services and facilities they will offer. Outside the United States, the brand's development will continue to focus on the European market.

Days Inn

Days Inn, which is directed at the lower- to midprice segment of the market, is the brand name with the biggest portfolio of all Cendant Corporation's different brands. Its hotels are located in the United States, Canada, China, Colombia, the Czech Republic, Hungary, Puerto Rico, Uruguay, India, Israel, Mexico, the Philippines, and South Africa. There are also plans to move into the Argentinean, Italian, Paraguayan, and Venezuelan markets, but this has not happened. Consequently the brand has been and continues to be one of Cendant Corporation's main vehicles for international growth.

In 2000, Days Inn announced a new hotel prototype to be applied to those hotels whose construction would begin as of April 2000. This new hotel design is characterized by distinguishing features such as inner corridors, breakfast areas, a swimming pool, and small conference rooms. One of its main peculiarities is that 25 percent of each hotel's rooms are suites.

Marriott Hotels, Resorts & Suites

Marriott Hotels, Resorts & Suites, a brand directed at the hotel industry's main markets, was Marriott International's highest range of brand until it took over Ritz-Carlton. Generally speaking, Marriott Hotels, Resorts & Suites are large-capacity hotels, with approximately 375 rooms per hotel, although the brand's four-star hotels are smaller and are located in secondary markets. The brand's top range hotels all have a "JW" at the beginning of their name.

Comfort Inn

Comfort Inns are hotels directed at the midrange segment, with limited services that normally include conference rooms and gymnasiums. Most do not have a restaurant in the hotel. Comfort Suites have bigger rooms, convention facilities, and free continental breakfasts, although in some cases they are similar to Comfort Inns. Choice Hotels International uses the expression "luxury at a reasonable price" to describe this brand.

Sheraton Hotels & Resorts

These are top range hotels in leading destinations, mainly in Germany. The brand also includes Arabella Sheraton hotels, which are of a similar category.

Super 8 Motels

Founded in 1974, Super 8 Motels was given this name because the brand's first hotel charged an ADR of $8.88. Of all Cendant Corporation's brands, this one has the greatest number of hotels.

Super 8 Motels are small, with an average of sixty-one rooms (i.e., with a minimum of sixteen rooms or a maximum of 300). The motels' target market consists of travelers with a limited budget, using their own car to travel. It has no subbrands and uses the simple formula "clean, friendly service." Most of its franchisees (62 percent) own more than one motel.[5]

Ramada Franchise Systems

Ramada Franchise Systems, founded in 1954, focuses on the mid and mid-to-high segment of the business market. Cendant Corporation holds the North American rights to this brand, while Marriott International holds them for the rest of the world. It has three subbrands: Ramada Plaza Hotel, Ramada Inn, and Ramada Limited.

Hampton Inn & Suites

These hotels, as the name indicates, combine traditional hotel rooms with suites with a residential flavor. The services offered include a continental breakfast buffet, local calls, a film channel, and free newspaper. Hilton Hotels Corporation's portfolio is largely made up of hotels belonging to this brand.

Express by Holiday Inn

Express hotels are designed to meet the requirements of the mid-price segment of the market, whether guests are traveling for business or pleasure. Mainly directed at the U.S. market, they are economically priced hotels with limited facilities and room rates below those of Holiday Inn hotels.

In 1998, Six Continents Hotels made some changes to Express by Holiday Inn, similar to other previous ones. For example, it separated the Crowne Plaza name from the hotel chain's main brand. The word "Express" was given special emphasis in marketing campaigns and, in representative symbols and logos and on a corporate basis, company representatives started to talk about the "Express" brand, indicating that the "Holiday Inn" prefix could gradually be phased out. This has still not happened. However, it seems likely, since Express has been extraordinarily successful in growth terms, mainly in the United States. The "Express" brand covers almost 85 percent of the main brand's hotels, although it accounts for a much lower percentage of rooms, because Express by Holiday Inn hotels are generally smaller than Holiday Inns. In October 1999, Express by Holiday Inn opened its one thousandth hotel. During the tax year that ended in September 2000, 6.5 times more Express hotels were opened than those belonging to other Holiday Inn brand names.

Radisson Hotels & Resorts

These are full-service hotels directed at the top end of the market, with convention and conference facilities. There are several sub-brands, although Carlson Hospitality Worldwide does not use them in all locations. They are Radisson Plaza Hotels, Radisson Suites Hotels, Radisson Resorts, Radisson SAS Hotels, and Radisson Edwardian.

Motel 6

Motel 6 belongs to Accor. This is a roadside motel chain, mainly located in the United States (with a limited presence, since 1999, in Toronto, Canada). Motel 6 competes directly with brands such as Travelodge and Days Inn, both belonging to Cendant Corporation. Based on a North American prototype for this type of hotel, most Motel 6 properties offer some leisure facilities, such as a swimming pool. All the rooms have a private bathroom, but there are no restaurants or communal lounges.

Hilton Hotels

Hilton Hotels are top-range hotels located in big business centers, major cities, airports, and tourist areas of the United States. The brand's flagships are the Waldorf Astoria, the Hilton Hawaiian Village Beach Resort and Spa, and the Palmer House Hilton. Whether traveling on business or for pleasure, clients using a Hilton Hotel should expect the experience to be special, thanks to the quality that these hotels offer.

After thirty-three years as separate entities and a lawsuit for undue use of the Hilton name, in 1997 both Hilton companies formed a marketing alliance. In mid-1998, they announced a new combined brand identity, because research had proved that the word "Hilton" has been and still is synonymous worldwide with the hotel trade.

Consequently, as already mentioned, wherever necessary the names of most Hilton hotels were changed in order to benefit from the prestige that is associated with this brand name. Thus Hilton became the first word, followed by other names indicative of the hotel itself (usually of a geographic nature). Some hotels with classic or historic names, such as the Waldorf Astoria in New York, kept their names to take advantage of their special status and their original brand name. This kind of standardization has been attempted before, not only by the two Hiltons but also by others. Nevertheless, owners fail when they demand that their choice of name is used.

Quality

Quality competes with brands such as Novotel, Ramada, and Holiday Inn. Quality Inns and Quality Hotels are full-service, midprice hotels, with a bar, restaurant, swimming pool, and shopping center. As well as offering the same services and facilities as Quality Inns, Quality Suites have two different room categories. Choice Hotels International positions this brand in the mid-to-high segment of the market.

Courtyard by Marriott

Courtyard by Marriott are three-star, moderately priced hotels, located in city centers and on the outskirts of cities. The hotels include a garden area with a swimming pool, an outdoor jacuzzi, gymnasium, coffee bar, and restaurant. This brand was created partly in response to the idea that the Holiday Inns were becoming outdated.

Mercure

These are two- to four-star hotels but, unlike Novotel and Sofitel, they are not standard hotels. With Mercure hotels, clients can be sure of finding comfort and all the necessary services; however, each hotel has a special charm and personality of its own. In the past, Accor representatives described them as hotels in the tradition of former "grand hotels," in prestigious locations and with a stylish character. Most were situated in cities, although this has changed. The brand's objective is "to offer a network of mid-range hotels, each with a unique architectural design, service and atmosphere" (www.accor.com). From 1995, other subbrands were added, which broadened the range of hotels covered by the Mercure name. These subbrands are Mercure Grand, at the top end of the market (which, according to Accor, is equivalent to Sofitel), described as offering "refined comfort"; Mercure Hotels, in the midrange segment (equivalent to Novotel), described as offering an "alternative service"; and finally Mercure Inns (equivalent to Ibis), presented as offering "simplicity."

Hyatt Regency

These deluxe hotels constitute both Hyatt companies' core brand. Hyatt Regency describes its hotels as "a hotel within a hotel" with spacious guest rooms and additional features such as bathrobes and hair dryers. A Hyatt Regency hotel "is a refreshing oasis for guests who desire a higher level of service and privacy" (www.hyatt.com).

Ibis

These hotels, offering limited services, are directed at business and vacation travelers. About half of the brand's hotels are located in city centers, in strategic and/or tourist locations, or close to airports. In 1993, Ibis merged with Arcade, one of the brands taken over by Accor when it bought Wagonlits. Arcade subsequently disappeared in 1995. In the same year the Urbis subbrand also started to be phased out.

Novotel

Novotel, the name with which Accor was founded, has been regarded as the company's leading brand. Novotels are three- or four-star hotels,[6] built according to a standard design, particularly the rooms' furnishings and bathroom design. They are positioned at the top of the midrange segment and are full-service hotels, located in cities and vacation destinations or close to airports and major motorways.

Table 12.2 shows the different brands belonging to the Top 10 hotel chains with the greatest number of rooms. Hilton Hotels Corporation and Marriott International are the hotel chains recorded in January 2000 as owning the brands worth the most money, valued at 1.319 billion dollars and 1.193 billion dollars, respectively. They hold fifty-eighth and sixtieth place in the list of the world's top-ranking companies with the most valuable brands.[7]

Marriott International is the only chain in the world Top 10 that is present in all segments of the market. InterContinental, Accor, Choice Hotels International, and Hilton Hotels Corporation have hotels in all segments except the super deluxe end of the market. In contrast,

TABLE 12.2. Brands Belonging to the World Top 10, 2002

Hotel Chain	Economically Priced Segment	Midprice Segment	Top-Range Segment	Super Deluxe Segment
Cendant Corporation	Super 8 Motels	Ramada		
	Villager Lodges	Howard Johnson		
	Days Inn	AmeriHost		
	Travelodge	Wingate Inns		
	Knights Inns			
Six Continents Hotels	Express by Holiday Inn	Forum Hotels	Crowne Plaza	
		Holiday Inn	Inter-Continental	
		Holiday Inn Select		
		Holiday Inn Garden Court		
		Holiday Inn Sun-Spree Resorts		
		Staybridge Suites		
Marriott International	Fairfield	Courtyard	Marriott	Ritz-Carlton
	TownePlace Suites	Residence Inn	New World	
	SpringHill Suites	Ramada	Renaissance	
			JW Marriott	
Accor	Ibis	Novotel	Sofitel	
	Formule 1/Etap	Mercure		
	Motel 6			
	Red Roof Inn			
Choice Hotels International	Sleep Inn	Quality	Clarion	
	Rodeway Inn	Comfort		
	Econo Lodge	MainStay Suites		
		Flag Choice		

TABLE 12.2 *(continued)*

Hotel Chain	Economically Priced Segment	Midprice Segment	Top-Range Segment	Super Deluxe Segment
Hilton Hotels Corporation	Hampton Inn	Hilton Garden Inns	Hilton	
			Conrad	
			Embassy Suites	
			Homewood Suites	
			Doubletree	
Best Western International		Best Western		
Starwood Hotels & Resorts Worldwide		Four Points	Sheraton	Luxury Collection/ St. Regis
			Westin	
			W	
Carlson Hospitality Worldwide		Country Inns & Suites	Radisson Hotels	Regent
Sol Meliá		Tryp Hotels	Meliá Hotels & Resorts	
		Sol Hotels & Resorts	Paradisus Resorts	

Starwood Hotels & Resorts Worldwide and Carlson Hospitality Worldwide lack hotels only at the bottom end of the market. Sol Meliá has no hotels in the extreme top and bottom segments, whereas Cendant Corporation has none in the top and super deluxe segments.

The midrange segment is the only one in which all the world's Top 10 hotel chains are positioned, with twenty-five brands. Of special relevance in this segment are Cendant Corporation (the former Six Continents Hotels) and Choice Hotels International. The Top 10 chains all have brands with very similar coverage of the economically priced and top-range segments. The super deluxe segment has only three brands, belonging to Marriott International, Starwood Hotels & Resorts Worldwide, and Carlson Hospitality Worldwide.

The hotel chains specializing in the midrange and lower-priced segments are the ones that have expanded the most worldwide. This is reflected by the world Top 10, because the chains directed at these segments are the ones situated in the top half of the list, i.e., Cendant Corporation Corporation, the former Six Continents Hotels, Marriott International, Accor, and Choice Hotels International, whereas the chains from the bottom half of the list, i.e., Starwood Hotels & Resorts Worldwide, Hilton Hotels Corporation, and Carlson Hospitality Worldwide, have centered their energies on the top-range and luxury segments. Indeed, only one of these four chains has a brand (Hampton Inn) in the lower-priced segment.

The world Top 10 have started to absorb luxury hotel chains, mainly for two reasons. First, luxury hotel chains find it difficult to position themselves without assistance, as was the case of Regent and Ritz-Carlton, because they did not have the marketing and distribution power that big chains have. Second, some big hotel chains, including Marriott International and Carlson Hospitality Worldwide, have understood how necessary it is to include luxury hotels in their portfolios, as a means of diversifying their risk.

It is also true that hotel chains positioned at the top end of the market have found themselves forced to introduce midrange brands, given the increasing demand for this type of hotel. This is the case of Hilton Hotels Corporation, which has created a new Garden Inns brand, and Starwood Hotels & Resorts Worldwide, with its Four Points brand.

Some hotel chain executives, such as those of InterContinental and Starwood Hotels & Resorts Worldwide, believe that the chain's name should not be included in the names of its hotels, because the brand gives the hotels recognition (i.e., Holiday Inn, Sheraton, Arabella, and Westin), rather than the name of the company.

Accor has a slightly surprising branding policy, as it prefers to use French names, even though some of them may seem inappropriate in international markets. Most hotel companies have tried to find names that are easy to understand and pronounce, normally choosing a name in English, the international language for travelers.

SUMMARY

Branding consists of brand name research, development, and implementation. One of the main objectives is to position a certain product and generate a sense of client loyalty. As such, branding is a strategy of major importance. In the hotel trade, branding has evolved over the course of time. Between the 1950s and 1960s, developing one single brand name was typical, whereas in the 1980s multi-branding burst onto the scene. Now groupings of brand names are becoming common. This chapter explored the phenomenon of branding in the hotel industry, concluding with an analysis of the twenty hotel brand names with the biggest room portfolios in the world, led by Best Western International, with over 300,000 rooms. We also looked at how the world's Top 10 hotel chains have positioned their brand names from the perspective of their room portfolios. One remarkable example is Marriott International, a hotel chain whose brand names are present in all segments of the market.

Chapter 13

The Internationalization-Globalization of Hotel Chains

THE THEORY

Current phenomena, such as the increasingly evident degree of international competition, the acceleration of technological innovations, the process of the European Union, the growing international relevance of Southeast Asian economies, free trade agreements among countries such as the United States, Canada, and Mexico or among Latin American countries, and the increasing integration of different international financial markets, clearly represent a breakaway from the form of international economic development that previously existed. These events act as a springboard for the growth policies of companies that wish to expand beyond their countries' frontiers.

The worldwide phenomenon of market globalization must not be ignored, as it is both the cause and consequence of company internationalization. This and the problems deriving from the management of the internationalization process are factors that require the attention of company executives, politicians, academics, and the media (Porter, 1986; Ohmae, 1991; Vernon-Wortzel and Wortzel, 1991).

A whole series of forces led to the globalization process, as shown in Figure 13.1.

The globalization of markets offers new opportunities for foreign diversification, giving access to new geographic markets as a result of fewer commercial barriers, greater ease of communication, and lower transport costs.

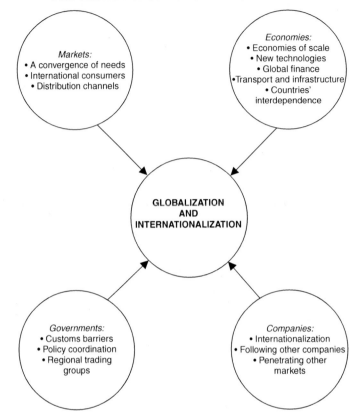

FIGURE 13.1. Forces That Lead to the Globalization of Markets

Nevertheless, other factors hinder the globalization of markets (see Figure 13.2):

- The markets themselves, due to national differences, derive from different market structures and different distribution systems.
- Governments can change the conditions of free market competition, altering exchange rates and promoting protectionist policies that support local businesses.
- Even within businesses themselves, qualified management personnel may be difficult to find and the operational structure may be barely developed.

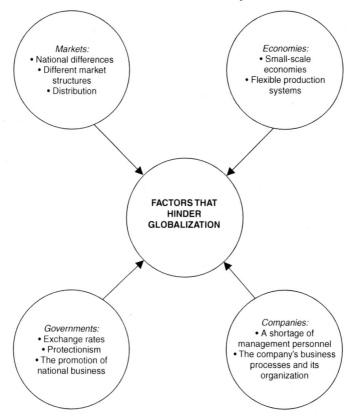

FIGURE 13.2. Factors That Hinder the Globalization of Markets

Globalization will pose the following new challenges for businesses:

- They will face the increasing presence of foreign businesses in local markets, representing further rivalry, greater price competition, and additional pressure to make continual improvements to the quality of products.
- Globalization involves added complexity for business management. Carrying out business operations in different geographic markets, with different clients, and with greater political, economic, and financial risks clearly represents a bigger challenge for management teams.
- Globalization also affects governments, as it imposes an increasing restriction on the design of their economic policies.

Strangely, examining the phenomenon of international competition reveals that the companies whose midterm business activities are dependent on international markets constantly strive to innovate and upgrade their products and processes.[1]

Different detrimental effects, such as currency appreciation, high interest rates, or a lack of official subsidies, can hinder businesses' internationalization. Nevertheless, a small sample of interviews between Jordi Canals and different Catalan company representatives with a desire for foreign expansion shows that it is not that these people are not worried about these factors, but rather that they simply do not believe them to be most significant (Canals, 1992). Two factors are stressed, however, to which they do lend importance: product quality, and wage costs versus productivity.

The importance of a product's quality reduces the significance of other supposedly critical factors, such as currency appreciation or a lack of official aid. If a company does not have a good product, neither a weak currency nor authorities who hand out generous amounts of aid to companies is much help. What is crucial is to offer high-quality products at reasonable prices.[2]

This leaves companies and authorities in a difficult position regarding what to do in the short term. The only possibility is further investment in qualified professional staff and applied research.

The other factor is the relationship between wage costs and productivity, i.e., not wage costs themselves, but the wage costs per product unit sold. Once again the subject of qualified professional staff is involved, since productivity rises more slowly when there is a shortage of qualified staff.

Two factors can be used to explain the process of internationalization: product quality or productivity. Both factors point toward the quality of the educational system as one of the determining factors in the successful internationalization and international competitiveness of a country's businesses.

In the past fifty years, tourism has had a profound effect on international social and economic development. The expansion of transnational tourism corporations was mainly attributable to the following factors:

- The emergence of new commercial centers throughout the world, especially in the Middle and Far East, and increasing competition among recently industrialized countries to become leading financial and commercial centers led to a boom in the construction of hotels and a big opportunity for tourism expansion by transnational corporations.
- Governments tend to play an important role in stimulating or restricting the growth of international tourism. A wide range of barriers exists that can limit worldwide travel, such as restrictions on the movement of people (visas), administrative delays (in obtaining licenses to begin building work or for the management of hotels by foreign hotel companies, for instance), and discrimination in favor of national businesses. On the other hand, government incentives can encourage many corporations involved in the tourism business to extend their activities to encompass these recently industrialized countries.[3]
- Most tourism-related international business transactions, including the transfer of capital, technology, management know-how, and cross-border operations, involve multinational or transnational corporations. Their travel infrastructure facilitates international tourism, especially to and within developing countries[4] (Ajami, 1988; McQueen, 1989).

Transnational corporations' expansion into the tourism business during the 1970s and 1980s can be explained by examining Dunning's eclectic paradigm. According to Dunning's international model of production, the magnitude, model, and growth of added-value activities undertaken by multinational companies outside their national limits are dependent on the value and interaction of three main variables: (1) the ownership-specific advantages of multinational firms; (2) the location-specific advantages of countries; and (3) market internalization or coordinating advantages (Dunning, 1981).

The term *ownership advantage* is used to refer to multinational corporations' competitive superiority over other national or foreign companies in the country in which this competition is taking place, and the multinationals' ability to combine activities in different geographic locations.

In the tourism industry, several specific reasons explain why multinationals have an ownership advantage:

- They can provide high-quality services, with the incorporation of features such as efficient design, comfort, good performance, professionalism, and a caring attitude to clients.[5]
- International hotel chains are able to penetrate new markets easily and swiftly, thanks to a series of intangible assets and logistical skills, which can be transferred to new hotels joining the chain at a lower cost than potential new entries into the hotel business by other rivals.
- International travelers generally tend to regard the availability of a global booking system as beneficial, making the reservation process much easier for them (UNCTC, 1988).

Next is an examination of countries' *location-specific advantages*.

As well as the previously mentioned advantages, executives of hotel and tourism corporations can also decide where to locate their added-value activities. A number of different variables determine whether a multinational hotel company will become involved in one country or another. Basically, these variables are similar to those of companies operating in other financial sectors. Examples include the size and growth rate of the demand, the local government's policy on foreign businesses, and the country's overall political, economic, and social stability (McQueen, 1989; Go et al., 1990).

Another crucial decision is where to locate a hotel within a chosen destination. Traditionally, inner-city hotels provide services for business travelers, while tourist resorts tend to attract vacationers. However, the distinctions are becoming blurred, as vacation hotels are attracting an increasing number of conventions, professional get-togethers, and congresses, whereas inner-city hotels deal mainly with business executives on weekdays but try to focus on the leisure market on weekends by offering discounts and special rates (Witt, Brooke, and Buckley, 1991).

A hotel's location within a vacation resort largely depends on the surrounding area, climate, and other leisure facilities sought by travelers. In addition to these general characteristics, other more specific factors also influence the location of hotels belonging to transnational tourism corporations (UNCTC, 1988). These include

- being close to markets of a considerable size, or guaranteed access to these markets with reasonable transport fares,

- the necessary organizational ability to adapt the products to the local infrastructure,
- being able to hire key members of staff at reasonable rates, and
- access to suppliers that provide a wide variety of products needed to run the hotels.

Regarding *market internalization* or *coordinating advantages,* since it is difficult to organize efficient markets of intermediary products in the tourist sector, hotel executives have a strong incentive to incorporate these markets into their organizational structure. This type of integration usually occurs when a company gains control of these resources by acquiring a shareholding or by entering into an alliance. With this process of integration, multinationals create their own internal markets, thereby increasing their power and efficiency in assigning resources (Dunning and McQueen, 1982; Litteljohn, 1985).

This propensity to enter into strategic alliances or agreements that do not involve the acquisition of share capital has been more prevalent in the service sector than in the industrial sector. By forming strategic alliances, transnational corporations have entered the hotel industry, the restaurant and catering sector, and the car rental business, thus controlling the key competitive advantages held by these service companies through management contracts or franchise agreements (UNCTC, 1988).

These include highly significant advantages such as the ensured quality of intermediate or end products, which is so crucial to those selling them. Thanks to the product's recognized brand name, any "buyer uncertainty" regarding the nature of the product is eliminated, as are bargaining costs and government intervention.

The key to the strategic management of any organization is the ability to adapt continually to a changing environment so as to survive or, even better, succeed (Dev and Olsen, 1989; West and Olsen, 1989). The environment in which a management team decides to operate and the team's attitude toward this environment can be based on one of five different approaches to international business:[6]

1. *Little or no interest in operating abroad.* Foreign operations are often seen as complicated and risky. The home market satisfies the management team's growth expectations.

For successive stages in the evolution of a company's process of internationalization, four other attitudes have been identified (Perlmutter, 1967).

2. *Ethnocentrism or a home-country orientation.* Some company leaders see foreign operations as an "appendix" to their home operations. Normally, companies that take this approach do not carry out extensive market analyses and do not adapt their promotional activities to operations in foreign markets.[7]

3. *Polycentrism or a host-country orientation.* Some company leaders set up subsidiaries for each foreign market. Often these subsidiaries are run by local staff from the same country so market activities tend to be planned and supervised nationally.

4. *Regiocentrism or a regional orientation.* Certain company executives confine their operations to a particular continental region such as North America (an area that includes the United States and Canada), i.e., with countries that have similar economies and cultures.[8]

5. *Geocentrism or a global orientation.* For some company leaders, the world market is their reference. Levitt sees strong benefits in companies that offer standard products on a global level that are advanced, functional, reliable, and cheap. He believes that only those companies that follow this global approach will be successful in the long term (Levitt, 1983).

Nevertheless, the global marketing approach defended by Levitt must be rejected, since it is the least desirable approach to take to tourism marketing, given countries' social and cultural differences. This approach should be combined with a sensitivity toward customs and local cultures (Ziff-Levine, 1990).

International hotel chain owners have developed a hub-and-spoke growth strategy, meaning that main "gateway" cities act as the central axis, while smaller, secondary destinations could be considered to represent the spokes. Traditionally, hotels positioned in gateway cities belong to hotel groups that use their top-range brand names to achieve a strong brand image (something that is enormously helpful when subscribing to new franchise or management contracts in secondary destinations in the midrange segment of the market).

A gateway city is a commercial center and a major administrative or political capital. Upmarket hotel companies have extended their networks in a similar fashion to airlines. Whereas an airline will add a new route, hotel companies will seek to position their brands in that type of destination.

The hub-and-spoke strategy has been applied by a large number of international hotel chains, mainly in emerging destinations. As an example we can cite Six Continents Hotels, which positioned itself in key cities in Asia via its Holiday Inn brand name, while Express by Holiday Inn was used in secondary cities. The most unusual case is Hilton International, with the strategy used to position itself in the United Kingdom. In London, Manchester, and Glasgow it expanded by using the Hilton International brand name, while using the Hilton Nationals name in smaller cities.

Of the Top 10 chains with the greatest number of rooms, InterContinental and Starwood Hotels & Resorts Worldwide have the greatest coverage of the world's leading gateway cities. Meanwhile, Cendant Corporation was planning to carry out an expansion program to penetrate Europe's leading gateway cities, but this has not happened. To do this, executives will have to use the Days Inn and Howard Johnson names, as the rights to Cendant's most prestigious international brand name, Ramada, are owned by Marriott International outside the United States. Next on the list is Best Western International, which is present in all of Europe's and America's leading gateway cities, although it is not well represented in other regions of the world. Marriott International, like Accor, is not present in all of the Asian continent's prime cities and, in Accor's case, the same is also true of the American continent.

Future additions to the ranks of the world's gateway cities will depend largely on the political stability and economic growth of the country in which each city is situated.

The emergence of a number of major businesses and tourist centers in North America is perhaps fairly predictable. Atlanta, for example, is the location of many corporate headquarters and is thus a prime candidate to become a gateway city. Miami's claim, meanwhile, has much to do with its tourist potential. Some cities in South America also seem likely to attract greater attention. Sao Paulo and Santiago are perhaps the strongest contenders. Other possibilities include Bogotá, but the level of crime in Colombia may be a limitation.

Similarly, development in some major cities in Eastern Europe may also be held back by problems with crime. Many hotel company leaders refuse to let their development teams into certain countries, such as Russia, due to the levels of corruption. In contrast, the growing economic power and political stability of cities such as Prague and Budapest make these highly likely candidates, particularly if their countries are admitted into the European Union.

In Asia, the most likely candidates are in China, thanks to its rapidly expanding economy. Similarly, Vietnam's Ho Chi Minh City has strong potential. In contrast, the current difficulties of the Japanese economy make Osaka a weaker candidate. Similarly, Indonesia's economic and political turmoil make both Surabaya and Jakarta less likely prospects.

Within a ten-year time frame, the potential maintenance or achievement of political stability is very hard to plot. It is particularly difficult in the Middle East. Here both Beirut and Jerusalem are strong candidates for gateway city status but only if peace is allowed to prevail.

Multinational tourism companies have also given rise to serious problems, particularly in countries that are tourist destinations. With the emergence of tourism, the residents of some such countries (particularly developing ones) often give up traditional employment in agriculture or industry to work in hotels, leading to a shortage of manpower in more traditional economic sectors. In transnational tourism companies' own interests, they should try to be more sensitive to matters that concern the host environment in which they operate.

EXAMPLES

Table 13.1 shows the ten hotel chains with the greatest international coverage in terms of the number of countries in which they operate. The Top 10 chains in terms of countries show significant differences in their coverage of countries. To make these differences clearer, we will divide them into four groups. The first contains one

TABLE 13.1. Companies Operating in the Most Countries, 2002

Companies	Countries
Six Continents Hotels	98
Accor	84
Starwood Hotels & Resorts Worldwide	82
Best Western International	80
Hilton Group PLC	68
Marriott International	65
Carlson Hospitality Worldwide	64
Le Méridien Hotels & Resorts	55
Golden Tulip Hotels, Inns & Resorts	46
Choice Hotels International	43

Source: www.hostelmag.com.

chain alone: InterContinental (formerly Six Continents Hotels). From the perspective of the number of countries in which it operated, Six Continents was clearly the world leader in internationalization in 2002, as it was present in ninety-eight countries. The second group is made up of hotel chains present in about eighty countries, including Accor, Starwood Hotels & Resorts Worldwide, and Best Western International. The third group is composed of hotel chains positioned in around sixty-five countries, including Hilton Group PLC, Marriott International, and Carlson Hospitality Worldwide. Le Méridien Hotels & Resorts are somewhere between the third and fourth groups, with hotels in fifty-five countries. The fourth group also consists of Golden Tulip Hotels, Inns & Resorts and Choice Hotels International, which are present in forty-six and forty-three countries, respectively.

Seven hotel chains from the Top 10 with the greatest number of hotel rooms also belong to the Top 10 present in the most countries. They are InterContinental, Marriott International, Accor, Choice Hotels International, Best Western International, Starwood Hotels & Resorts Worldwide, and Carlson Hospitality Worldwide. The Top 10 in terms of countries is completed by Hilton Group PLC, Le Méridien Hotels & Resorts, and Golden Tulip Hotels, Inns & Resorts.

For the past fifteen years Sheraton, Accor, Best Western International, and InterContinental have all figured among the ranks of the chains with the greatest degree of internationalization, in terms of the number of countries in which they operate. Sheraton headed this particular Top 10 in the late 1980s and early 1990s, with hotels in sixty-one countries. Accor took over from 1991 to 1993, with coverage of sixty-six countries. A year later, Sheraton regained the lead, with hotels in a total of sixty-four countries, but in 1995 and 1996 the French company once again reached the top of the list, positioning itself in sixty-eight countries in 1995 and seventy the following year. In 1997, Best Western International ranked first, with coverage of seventy-seven countries, and in 1998 it was Six Continents Hotels, which has been the unrivaled leader of this particular Top 10 until the present day, with hotels in almost 100 countries.

Group One

InterContinental

This is the hotel chain with the greatest worldwide coverage, with hotels in almost 100 countries. If the company's portfolio was shown as representing 100 rooms, it would have seventy in North America, thirteen in Europe, six in Asia, five in Central and South America, three in the Middle East, and another three in Africa.

In North America it has almost 2,450 hotels. Most are in the United States (2,286), but there are also 100 in Canada and sixty in Mexico. In Europe it has almost 410 hotels, mainly in the United Kingdom (with 103), Germany (seventy-four), and France (sixty-eight). In Germany it is expanding into the top end of the hotel market, through an association between InterContinental and Dorint. As InterContinental is present in twenty-eight European countries, this is the most important region for the company in terms of its coverage of countries. It has 115 hotels in Asia, mostly in China (with thirty-three) and Japan (twenty-one). In Central America and South America it has a total of seventy-four hotels, only fourteen more hotels than in Mexico. It has sixty-three hotels in the Middle East, principally in Saudi Arabia (with eighteen) and Israel (eleven). When Six Continents PLC and InterContinental's figures become more stable, InterContinental will become the region's leading operator. In Africa it has fifty-six hotels, mostly in South Africa (with thirty-seven) and Zimbabwe (six).

Group Two

Accor

Of all the companies belonging to the world Top 10 with the greatest number of rooms, Accor has the highest degree of internationalization, equivalent to 72 percent of its portfolio. If Accor's portfolio is represented as 100 rooms, it has forty-nine rooms in Europe, thirty-five in North America, eight in Asia, four in Latin America and the Caribbean, three in Africa, and one in the Middle East (Cunill, 2002).

It has 1,835 European hotels. Most are located in France (1,203), followed at a distance by Germany (248) and the United Kingdom (ninety-five). These three countries alone account for almost 85 percent of all the company's European hotels. The twenty-five European countries in which Accor is present make this the most important region in terms of its coverage of countries.

Even so, in Santiago de Compostela the French group presented an ambitious plan for Spanish expansion that actively involves each of its different business operations, with the hotel business as its nucleus. If Accor currently operates fifteen hotels in Spain, by 2004 this figure will have risen to 146 hotels. The hotels will be run under the Sofitel, Novotel, Mercure, Ibis, and Formule 1 brand names. Most will be located in inner-city areas such as Madrid, Barcelona, Valencia, Malaga, Bilbao, and Murcia. However, Accor also has well-advanced plans for coastal areas such as Marbella and Mojácar. According to the company chairman, the group plans to lease 60 percent of the hotels included in the project, while retaining ownership of the other 40 percent. Accor executives use a refinancing system. This means that, whenever possible, they sell the hotel once built, while retaining control of its management.[9]

Accor has 1,200 hotels in North America, mostly in the United States, with a total of 1,194. The other six are in Canada, and it has no hotels in Mexico. In the Asia-Pacific region it has 173 hotels, with ninety in Australia and twenty-four in Indonesia. In Latin America and the Caribbean it has a total of 125 hotels, most of which are located in Brazil (ninety-one). The ten remaining Latin American and Caribbean countries in which Accor is present have a maximum of forty hotels. In the Middle East, it has twenty-eight hotels, mainly in Israel (with eight).

In Argentina, Accor plans to expand by developing three-star hotels through its Ibis hotel chain. To carry out this project, the French company has joined forces with Bomagra, a firm belonging to the Argentinean entrepreneur Jorge Born. The company's objective is to open fourteen new hotels under the Ibis brand name within a five-year period. An estimated 4 million dollars are expected to be invested in each hotel, which will have an average of eighty-five rooms. Meanwhile, Accor plans to open a five-star hotel in Buenos Aires under its Sofitel brand name, requiring investment of about 30 million dollars (Cunill, 2002).

In addition to its Argentinean projects, Accor has others planned for Peru and the Dominican Republic. In Peru, after the recent inauguration of the eighty-one–room "Sofitel Royal Park" in Lima, Accor plans to open another new hotel: the "Novotel Cusco." Accor's plans for the Dominican Republic include the creation of 3,000 hotel rooms in ten different hotels located all over the country. As of December 2003, it had only seven hotels. For the French company's ambitious Latin American expansion program, investment of 450 million dollars is anticipated between 2002 and 2003.

According to company sources, between 2002 and the end of 2003 Accor aims to invest 270 million dollars in integrating seventy-one new hotels and apartment hotels located in the Mercosur economic area. At present Accor has 103 hotels and apartment hotels under six brand names. For the new hotels, 2,700 members of staff will need to be hired (Cunill, 2002).

Africa is a strange case, as it is the region with the greatest coverage in terms of countries, with 103 hotels in twenty-six different countries. Even so, Accor hopes to increase the number of hotels in the region, particularly in Tunisia, as the firm plans to triple its hotels there over five years, reaching a figure of 15,000 beds. As of December 2003, it had 15,390 rooms. Leaders have set up an investment company called STI[10] in conjunction with a group of local business entrepreneurs. STI, which the French company has a 35 percent stake in, will have access to finance of over 81 million euros for the construction of new hotels or the integration of existing ones under management contracts. Assisting Accor in the project is THR/Accor Gestión, a firm that coordinates Accor's management activities in Tunisia. STI has a 27.5 percent stake in THR/Accor Gestión.

Starwood Hotels & Resorts Worldwide

This American company has the greatest worldwide coverage in terms of countries. It is present in eighty-two countries, with a degree of internationalization of 37 percent (i.e., with 268 hotels outside the United States).

If Starwood Hotels & Resorts Worldwide's portfolio is represented as 100 rooms, it has sixty-six in North America (all in the United States); thirteen in Asia and the Pacific; nine in Europe; eight in the Middle East, India, and Africa; and four in Latin America (Cunill, 2002).

It has a total of 455 hotels in North America, all in the United States. Starwood Hotels & Resorts Worldwide will manage fourteen of the sixteen hotels bought by Grubarges from Bedrock Partners for 325 million dollars.[11] Until now, the sixteen hotels formed part of the Garden division of the Wyndham chain.

It has 105 hotels in Europe, mainly in Italy (with twenty-eight) and Germany (twenty-one). Almost 50 percent of all its European hotels are located in these two countries alone. The twenty-two European countries in which Starwood Hotels & Resorts Worldwide operates make it the company's most important region in terms of its coverage of countries.

It has eighty-three hotels in the Asia-Pacific region, primarily in Australia and China (with twelve hotels) and Indonesia (eleven), although it operates in a total of nineteen countries. It has thirty-five hotels in the Middle East, mainly in Israel (eleven), Saudi Arabia (eight), and the United Arab Emirates (seven). These three countries alone account for practically 70 percent of all its Middle Eastern hotels. It has twenty-three hotels in Africa, with nine in Egypt and four in Morocco. In Latin America it has a total of twenty-two hotels in ten different countries, with most of its hotels (seven) in Argentina. Despite this, Starwood Hotels & Resorts Worldwide plans to expand in

Brazil, Chile, and Mexico, mainly in secondary cities. The chain has taken over the Hotel Internacional in Iguazú (Argentina).

Best Western International

Over half of Best Western International's hotels are located in international markets. To facilitate its international expansion, the consortium has opened twenty-eight associate offices around the world. The most recent one was opened in Sydney in 2000.

If Best Western International's portfolio is shown as representing 100 rooms, it has sixty-seven in North America, twenty-six in Europe, four in Asia and the Pacific, two in Latin America, and one covering the Middle East, the Caribbean, and Africa (Cunill, 2002).

In North America it has a total of 2,345 hotels. These are distributed as follows: 2,123 in the United States, 162 in Canada, and 60 in Mexico.

It has 1,252 European hotels, mainly in the United Kingdom (with 344), France (191), and Germany (131). The forty European countries in which Best Western International is present make this the region where it has the greatest coverage in terms of countries.

It has a total of 377 hotels in the Asia-Pacific region, mostly in Australia (with 276) and New Zealand (sixty-eight). It has sixty-nine hotels in Latin America, mainly in Brazil (with eighteen) and Chile (fourteen). The company has fourteen hotels in the Middle East, including five in Israel. In this region it is present in only six countries.

Group Three

Hilton Group PLC

Seventy-eight percent of Hilton Group PLC's hotels are situated outside the United Kingdom, as almost 48,000 of its 61,000 rooms are located in international markets. If its portfolio were to take the form of 100 rooms, it would have forty-four in Europe, twenty-two in Asia and the Pacific, nine in Latin America and the Caribbean, eleven in Africa, seven in the Middle East, and another seven in North America (Cunill, 2002).

The company has 125 hotels in Europe, with a total of eighty-three in the United Kingdom and Ireland. In the other sixteen European countries where Hilton Group PLC is present, it has less than ten hotels per country. It has thirty-two hotels in Asia and the Pacific, one-quarter of which are in Australia. The Hilton Group has twenty-five hotels in Africa, primarily in Egypt (with twelve) and Kenya (four), with coverage of ten of the region's countries. Hilton Group PLC has a total of seventeen hotels in Latin America and the Caribbean, with three hotels in Brazil and three in Venezuela. It has thirteen hotels in the Middle East, with seven in the United Arab Emirates and coverage of just four countries. It has thirteen North American hotels, mainly in Canada (with eleven). The two remaining hotels are in the United States.

Marriott International

The Marriott International hotel chain has almost 93,000 rooms in international markets, representing 23 percent of its hotel portfolio. If its portfolio is shown as being equivalent to 100 rooms, it has seventy-eight in North America, ten in Europe, six in Asia and the Pacific, four in Latin America and the Caribbean, and two in the Middle East and Africa (Cunill, 2002).

It has 1,936 hotels in North America, mostly in the United States (with 1,900). The remaining thirty-six hotels are either in Canada (with twenty-seven) or Mexico (with nine).

It has 175 European hotels, primarily in Germany (with sixty-nine) and the United Kingdom (fifty-nine). These two countries represent almost three-quarters of Marriott International's European hotels. The seventeen European countries in which Marriott International is present make Europe the most important region in terms of its coverage of different countries, together with Latin America and the Caribbean. Even so, its presence is far less significant than that of chains such as Best Western International, with hotels in forty European countries.

It has seventy hotels in Asia and the Pacific, most of which are in China (with twenty-two). Marriott International's goal was to end the year 2002 with eighty-seven hotels and over 33,000 rooms, introducing six brand names to thirteen of the region's countries. In doing so,

Marriott International would increase its number of hotels in Asia and the Pacific by 15 percent and its rooms by 10 percent. At the same time, leaders also planned to open their first hotel in Taiwan in early 2005 in the city of Taipei, under a franchise agreement with Yihwa International Corporation, a company whose major shareholder is the Taipei Brickyard Corporation. As of December 31, 2004, Marriott had only seventy-three hotels and 26,682 rooms in the Asia-Pacific region.

Finally, it has twenty-four hotels in the Middle East and Africa, with six in the United Arab Emirates and coverage of eight of the region's countries. In Latin America, Marriott International has a total of thirty hotels (just three more hotels than it has in Canada), with four in Brazil.

The company's chairman, J.W. Marriott Jr., declared that: "by late 2004, the company's portfolio will be made up of 41 hotels, offering 13,259 rooms and six brand names in 21 of the region's countries."[12] As of December 31, 2004, it had not happened. At the same time, the U.S. hotel chain has subscribed to an agreement with a local tourist operator to program thirty-four charter flights from Europe.

Carlson Hospitality Worldwide

Carlson Hospitality Worldwide has 53,500 rooms outside the United States, equivalent to 40 percent of its portfolio. If Carlson Hospitality Worldwide's portfolio is represented as 100 rooms, it has sixty-five in North America, twenty-one in Europe, nine in Asia and the Pacific, three in Latin America and the Caribbean, one in the Middle East, and one in Africa (Cunill, 2002).

Carlson Hospitality Worldwide has 554 hotels in North America, mostly in the United States (with 511 hotels). The other forty-three hotels are distributed as follows: thirty-six in Canada and seven in Mexico.

It has 136 hotels in Europe, primarily in Norway (with twenty-two hotels), Germany (twenty), Sweden (eighteen), and the United Kingdom (fourteen). These countries represent over half of Carlson Hospitality Worldwide's European hotels. The twenty-three European countries in which the company is present make this the most important region in terms of Carlson's coverage of countries.

It has forty-three hotels in Asia and the Pacific, mostly in Australia (with eleven) and Indonesia (seven), with coverage of fourteen of the region's countries. In Latin America, Carlson Hospitality Worldwide has nineteen hotels. No particular country stands out from the rest, as the company has a maximum of two hotels in each Latin American country where it is present. It has seven hotels in the Middle East and, like the previous region, it is not more strongly present in any particular country. The company has penetrated the African continent for the first time, with two new hotels in Mauritania and South Africa.

Group Four

Le Méridien Hotels & Resorts

Le Méridien Hotels & Resorts is an almost fully internationalized hotel chain, as 120 of its 138 hotels are located in international markets, outside the United Kingdom. If its portfolio were to take the form of 100 rooms, it would have forty-four in Europe, seventeen in Asia and the Pacific, fourteen in the Middle East, thirteen in Africa, seven in North America, and five in Latin America (Cunill, 2002).

The company has sixty-one hotels in Europe, primarily in the United Kingdom (with eighteen), Germany (six), and Italy (six). The nineteen European countries in which it is present make this the most important region in terms of the chain's coverage of countries. It has twenty-four hotels in Asia, most of which are located in Thailand (with five hotels). In the Middle East it has nineteen hotels, with six in the United Arab Emirates. In Africa it has eighteen hotels, with three in the Seychelles. In North America it has a total of nine hotels, mainly in the United States (seven). In Latin America and the Caribbean it has seven hotels, with five in the French West Indies.

Golden Tulip Hotels, Inns & Resorts

Three quarters of Golden Tulip's portfolio, or 185 of its 245 hotels, are located in international markets outside Holland. If Golden Tulip Hotels, Inns & Resorts' portfolio is represented as 100 rooms, it has eighty-six in Europe, four in Latin America, four in the Middle East, and the remaining six cover North America, Africa, and Asia and the Pacific (Cunill, 2002).

It has 210 hotels in Europe, primarily in Holland (with sixty), Norway (thirty-five), and France (twenty-eight). The nineteen European countries in which Golden Tulip Hotels, Inns & Resorts is present make this the most important region in terms of its coverage of countries. It has a total of eleven hotels in Latin America and the Caribbean, with five in Brazil. Likewise, it also has eleven hotels in the Middle East, with three in Israel and Jordan. In North America it has five, with three in the United States and the other two in Canada. It also has five hotels in Africa in an equal number of countries. In Asia it has three hotels in China, Indonesia, and Thailand.

Choice Hotels International

One-quarter of Choice Hotels International's portfolio is located abroad, i.e., 91,000 rooms. If its portfolio is shown as representing 100 rooms, it has eighty in North America, twelve in Europe, seven in the Asia-Pacific region, and one covering Latin America, the Caribbean, the Middle East, and Africa (Cunill, 2002).

It has over 3,550 hotels in North America, mostly in the United States, where there are 3,300 hotels. The rest (almost 250 hotels) are all in Canada. The chain no longer runs its fifteen Mexican hotels. It has 435 hotels in Europe, with 122 in France, eighty-seven in the United Kingdom, and sixty-seven in Norway. These three countries account for almost two-thirds of the company's European hotel portfolio. As Choice Hotels International is present in thirteen European countries, this is the region where it has the greatest coverage in terms of countries. Nevertheless, its presence is far inferior to chains such as Best Western International, which operates in forty European countries. In the Asia-Pacific region, it has 455 hotels, primarily in Australia (339 hotels) and New Zealand (seventy-six). These two countries possess 91 percent of Choice Hotels International's Asia-Pacific portfolio. In the remaining regions, Latin America, the Caribbean, the Middle East, and Africa, the American multinational has only twenty-eight hotels.

SUMMARY

This chapter explored the forces behind market globalization and possible constraints. It examined Dunning's eclectic paradigm, according to which the magnitude, model, and growth of added value activities undertaken by multinational companies outside their national limits are dependent on the value and interaction of three main variables: (1) the ownership-specific advantages of multinational firms; (2) the location-specific advantages of countries; and (3) market internalization or coordinating advantages. In continuation, we examined five approaches to international business, ranging from little or no interest in operating abroad to geocentrism or a global orientation. The theory section concluded by highlighting the key role the hub-and-spoke strategy has played in international hotel expansion. Last, an analysis was made of the internationalization-globalization of the world's 10 most globalized hotel chains in terms of their coverage of different countries.

Notes

Chapter 2

1. There may be factors of tactical relevance. However, the main focus of an analysis of the structure of an industrial sector is the ability to identify the sector's main characteristics, which are deeply rooted in its economic and technological environment, as they are the foundations on which a competitive strategy is based.

2. This type of strategy makes the company particularly vulnerable to all disturbances that lead to an increase in costs.

3. It is important to emphasize that differentiating a company's products, customer care, technology, quality, etc., acts as an entry barrier or as a defense against the competition. The degree of differentiation can be reduced by rival imitations, changes in consumer preferences, or an imbalance between the "price premium" and the exact nature of the differentiation introduced.

4. The market niche strategy means that a company will position itself in relation to its strategic target in such a way that it can operate at a low cost or with a high degree of differentiation, or both. This strategy can also be used to choose targets that are less vulnerable to possible substitute products or in situations in which the company's rivals are weaker.

5. We should mention that different studies have revealed a correlation among profitability, competitive strategies, and a company's market share. Writing on the subject, Porter says that companies that adopt cost leadership strategies also have a high market share and high profit levels. Those that try to use differentiation or market niche strategies also achieve high profit levels, but they have a lower market share. Companies in a mid position achieve low profit levels that will gradually situate them in an unfavorable position.

6. The area for this brand name is limited. Granada Compass Hotels holds the rights to the brand name in Europe, the Middle East, and Africa; SPHC Hotels holds them for Asia and the Pacific.

7. Hilton Hotels Corporation could be described as a *historic business enterprise,* as it has been *innovative* in several different ways: it was the first nationwide hotel chain in the United States; the first hotel company to be listed on the stock exchange; and the first chain to offer direct-dial telephones and air-conditioning in its rooms as a standard amenity. From a commercial point of view, it can be distinguished from the rest thanks to its pioneering role as a hotel franchiser. What all this means is that the company has a know-how and spirit of innovation that far exceeds that of other hotel chains.

8. Wingate Inn competes directly with Marriott International's Courtyard Hotels and Hilton Hotel Corporation's Hampton Hotels.

Chapter 3

1. An internationalization strategy must not be construed as always representing an alternative to a diversification strategy. In many cases, internationalization accompanies and assists a diversification strategy.

2. The corporation has over 40,000 employees with offices in about 100 countries and a portfolio of over 100 million clients.

3. This company rents one car every two seconds.

4. Founded in 1946, PHH Vehicle Management Services purchases vehicles and offers a consultancy and vehicle-leasing service to companies, public institutions, etc. PHH's income is therefore derived from vehicle rentals and from its company management and consultancy fees.

5. These are distributed as follows: 1,400 properties in the United States and Canada; 1,260 in Europe and Africa; 475 in Mexico and Latin America; and 320 on the Asian continent and the Pacific. It also has properties in Australia.

6. Century 21 buys or sells a house every minute of the day.

7. If an employee must relocate for professional reasons, the real estate agency sells his or her house and searches for a new one.

8. The services offered by Accor's service division are used by over 14 million people in thirty-four countries. The group designs the services concept and management system for companies and public bodies.

9. Steven Bollenbach is the first person in the history of Hilton Hotels Corporation to be a company chairman and not bear the surname Hilton.

10. With this acquisition, the company became the biggest casino firm in the world.

11. In the third quarter of 2002, Marriott International completed a strategy of Senior Living Services business. However, Marriott decided to exit that business.

12. Club Med was actually created by a tour operator and not by a traditional hotel company.

Chapter 4

1. For examples see Morvan (1985) and Jacquemin (1982). Also see a brief account in Martinet (1983).

2. This theory encapsulates most of the arguments in favor of vertical disintegration.

3. The TUI Group has subsidiaries and shareholdings in all continents of the world. The company controls over fifty tour operator brand names and nearly 3,500 travel agencies. It has a fleet of seventy-eight planes and shareholdings in over 180 hotels, mostly through Grupotel and Riu. It is the biggest European tourism group, with over 80,000 beds, and it also owns the English Thomas Cook brand name. The consortium has a workforce of 56,000 people and in 2002 it made a turnover of almost 21,600 million euros, 51 percent of which was made by its tourism division.

4. In September 1997, Preussag acquired 99.2 percent of a Hamburg-based transport and tourism company with a 150-year history in business and a record as a world leader in tourism, transport, and logistics. This company was Hapag Lloyd, with its travel agencies, cruise lines, and airline companies. In 1998 Preussag in-

creased its shareholding of TUI, the biggest European tour operator, to 50.1 percent. In 1999, Preussag took over the biggest German chain of travel agencies, First, and at the same time it acquired full ownership of TUI. The German consortium's latest acquisition was its purchase of the huge British tour operator Thompson.

5. The big German tour operators are also investing heavily in the hotel sector. The reason is simple: it is a profitable business that also enables the tour operator to own its own hotel beds in popular destinations (such as the Spanish and Greek islands) and to dictate prices. Likewise, it leads to the closure of rival hotels (this is what Riu, owned by TUI, forced C&N to do, and Iberostar, owned by C&N, forced TUI to do).

6. Airtours is Britain's leading tour operator and the world's second largest after Preussag. During the 2002 financial year it made a turnover of over 6 billion euros, with a gross profit of more than 252.4 million euros. With a total of 20,000 employees, it is present in seventeen countries. Its main shareholder is the North American company Carnival, which owns 26 percent of its share capital. Globally it has ninety-three hotels (fifty-three of which are in Spain), and 48,000 hotel beds (31,400 in Spain).

7. The chain, belonging to the Spanair-Marsans group, currently has a total of fifty-seven hotels, with about 13,000 rooms and over 15,000 beds. There are eight hotels in Majorca, five in Lanzarote, four in Cuba, and three in the Dominican Republic.

8. The company has a total of 2,040 moorings in 485 ports, employing over 1,500 workers.

9. The cruise market is currently undergoing a period of expansion, as only 7 percent of the North American population have been on a cruise. This represents a great opportunity for the future development of the market.

10. The agreement authorizes First Choice's integration of all the companies belonging to the Viajes Barceló division on a nationwide and international level. The new integrated group would be given all the minority shares that Barceló Viajes owns in other companies and business groups.

11. After taking over Ten Tours, the British tour operator's executives indicated that their objective was to position the tour operator in the European market, improve its productivity, and increase its clients by 25 percent to over 5 million.

12. Galileo International was created by eleven companies. These are the North American and European airlines Aer Lingus, Air Canada, Alitalia, Austrian Airlines, British Airways, KLM Royal Dutch Airlines, Olympic Airways, Swissair, TAP, United Airlines, and US Airways. Galileo International uses a sales network and marketing team that include employees of Galileo and distributors operating in 107 countries throughout the world. This organizational structure requires in-depth knowledge of the local conditions of the travel industry.

13. The Iberia Group will increase the number of seats that are filled on its planes by directing its efforts at the big increase in middle-class Spanish tourism that has occurred over the past few years, thanks to the period of economic growth. Meanwhile, Sol Meliá will be able to increase the occupancy of its hotels, thus continuing to reduce the seasonality of its activities, thanks to the increase in demand during the off-season.

14. According to one study by Júpiter MMXI, Lastminute.com, with 3 million subscribers, is the most visited travel portal in the United Kingdom and France.

Lastminute (the result of agreements made with over 9,000 worldwide suppliers) offers clients the possibility of last-minute offers for plane tickets, hotel rooms, holiday packages, and other products and services.

Chapter 5

1. Following a traditional approach, management duties include planning, organizing, leading, coordinating, and controlling.

2. With divisionalized and diversified companies, there is almost certainly a potential for management, commercial, and financial synergies, which will clearly impact their growth policy and, therefore, their size if put to good use.

3. Ten European tour operators control 70 percent of the market.

4. During this period, its lower-capacity hotels had an average of 109 rooms each.

5. These companies are also the Top 10 leaders in terms of the number of hotels they own, except for Sol Meliá, whose position is occupied by the French chain Société du Louvre.

6. On December 31, 1999, they either fully owned, leased, or had management or franchise agreements for 716 hotels in seventy countries on five continents, with a total of 270,000 rooms. Starwood Hotels & Resorts Worldwide had gone from virtual anonymity to one of the international luxury hotel business's elite group of companies.

7. Vivendi consisted of fifty-two hotels, mostly in Paris, belonging to the Demeure and Libertel brand names.

8. However, operations are not always successful. For example, executives of the British chain Thistle were forced to throw in the towel when they were unable to find a buyer prepared to pay 1.3 billion pounds (sterling) for its assets. Instead, owners had to sell about thirty hotels to get sufficient liquidity and recover from its huge stock market drop as a result of the fiasco.

Chapter 6

1. Through its subsidiary, Grucysa, FCC would be responsible for the construction of new hotels which would then become part of the hotel chain. Meanwhile, Argentaria would deal with the financing of operations, also providing the real estate, and Barceló would run the hotels.

Chapter 7

1. In effect, due to a surplus of hotel accommodation at the end of the 1980s, hotel companies or developers did not focus their attention on building new hotels, because they could buy existing premises at 70 percent of their real value.

2. Starwood Lodging Trust and Patriot American (which emerged from virtually nowhere) have become two of the most important hotel companies with a large number of well-known brand names (Sheraton, Westin, etc.).

3. The traditional REITs are legally entitled to purchase hotels, but they are not allowed to manage them. Instead they must offer a leasing contract to other companies, whereas paired-shared REITs were allowed to combine real estate transactions with the management of hotels, benefiting from a special tax status.

4. However, we can already find examples, such as the acquisition of the French chain Vivendi by the Accor group (after the Spanish company Sol Meliá bid for it).

5. Whitbread PLC has companies that manufacture and distribute wine, beer, and spirits. It also owns and runs hotels, restaurants, and pubs. In the 2002 financial year (closing on February 28) their sales totaled more than 2.9 billion pounds.

6. Swallow has thirty-six hotels in some of England's and Scotland's foremost cities. During the 2002 financial year, it achieved a sales figure of 284 million pounds.

7. Century International Hotels has sixteen hotels and 5,300 hotel rooms in six countries: China and Hong Kong, Indonesia, Singapore, Malaysia, the Philippines, and Vietnam.

8. Zenith Hotels International has six hotels and over 1,600 rooms in China's main cities.

9. The German chain has forty-six hotels in Germany (where it is the third biggest hotel operator), six in Austria, and one in Switzerland. All its hotels are run under leaseholds, except for one.

Chapter 8

1. The brand names are Doubletree, Embassy Suites, Homewood, and Hampton Inn & Suites.

2. This alliance is particularly interesting because Friendly PLC originally formed part of the said hotel chain.

3. This is a 50/50 joint venture between Choice Hotels International and UniHost, a company that was formed in 1993 when UniHost grouped all its hotels under the Choice Hotels International name in order to create the biggest hotel chain in Canada: Choice Hotels Canada.

4. Flag Choice Hotels, a wholly owned subsidiary of Flag International Limited, acquired a twenty-year master franchise from Choice Hotels International to use the Clarion, Quality, and Comfort brand names, with option rights for an additional ten years. Flag Choice also manages Clairon's booking system and the marketing operations of Flag's current chain in Australia, Fiji, New Zealand, and Papua New Guinea: regions where it owns almost 340 hotels and 20,000 hotel rooms. Under the terms of the new agreement, some Flag hotels have changed brand names and been added to Choice Hotels International's portfolio of brand names.

Chapter 9

1. A study of franchising trends, carried out for the International Franchising Association (IFA) by the Naisbitt Group, shows that annual growth rates in brand or product franchising have decreased considerably. In the future, they are expected to level out or decrease even further.

2. According to a study published by the U.S. Department of Trade in 1990, sales made through business-format franchising increased from 192.4 billion dollars in 1988 to 213 billion in 1990.

3. This is the case of operations carried out by McDonalds, Choice Hotels International, Radio Shack, etc.

4. In 1990, 34 percent of all retail sales were made by franchisees operating under this kind of system.

5. In the case of North America, the franchisee must also obtain information on the company's disclosure document, following initial negotiations and contact with representatives of the company. This document, which is mandatory under U.S. federal and state laws, obliges franchisers to make a statement notifying potential franchisees of the company's background and the way in which it operates. These declarations must include all the information that a franchisee needs to know about a franchiser. This information must familiarize the franchisee with the company's organization and operating methods. When in doubt, the franchisee must always ask the franchiser's representative, who must clarify any gray areas.

6. The introduction of know-how is an essential part of the system, because the franchiser's full knowledge of its own business is transferred to the franchisee. This know-how, which requires constant updates, must be encapsulated in franchise manuals or in "bibles," as these documents are commonly known in the industry.

7. However, the company has designed a number of plans of action that offer almost guaranteed success. For example, 95 percent of Days Inn's franchisees renew their franchise contracts, which is very significant if we consider that this brand name covers over 1,900 hotels. It should also be emphasized that 62 percent of Super 8's franchisees have more than one franchise.

8. Through 2008 the company plans to develop fourteen hotels in Great Britain under this brand name.

9. In July 2000, Days Inn leaders signed a master franchise agreement with Hotelpage.com, entitling the latter to use the brand name in the Republic of Korea. The aim of the agreement was to develop twenty hotels by 2005. In September 2000, they signed another master franchise agreement with Bruno Petruzzo and Andrea Cesaretti to develop the brand name in Italy through a number of midrange hotels. The agreement covers a period of twenty years.

10. A franchise contract signed in Chile in the mid-1990s covers Chile, Peru, Bolivia, and Ecuador, and the franchisee agreed to develop forty hotels in the region within a period of ten years. Another franchise contract covers Argentina, Paraguay, and Uruguay, aimed at developing thirty-five hotels within a period of ten years. A third example is Brazil, where an agreement has been reached to have seventy-five hotels in operation there within a similar period of time.

11. The Profit Manager system synchronizes each hotel's occupancy data with the Choice 2001 system, meaning that sales agents can sell every one of each hotel's available rooms. This system includes a revenue management option, which calculates and suggests optimum room rates and an ideal length of stay based on each hotel's past operations and on its planned occupancy figures.

12. One of TSP's basic components is a hardware rental agreement for Dell Computers through a subsidiary of the company called Choice Hotels International Services Corp. The latter rents the hardware and then re-rents it to franchisees. For

the franchisees, the advantage is an absence of initial costs and the fact that the business's technology is updated periodically.

13. This system has been quite successful: 75 percent of franchisees use it regularly. Indeed, in January and February 2001, there was an increase of 44 percent compared to the whole of the year 2000. It commercializes more than 200,000 products and services.

14. The franchiser and franchisee are entitled, under certain conditions, to terminate the agreement before its twentieth year has passed.

15. Generally, master franchise contracts have a minimum duration of ten years. The company has subscribed to agreements of this type only for hotels franchised outside the United States.

Chapter 10

1. "Negotiating International Hotel Chain Management Agreements. A Primer for Hotel Chain Owners in Developing Countries." United Nations Center on Transnational Corporations. New York, 1990, pp. 4-11.

2. For example, Hilton Hotels Corporation sold 50 percent of six of its biggest hotels to the Prudential Insurance Company of America in 1975 for over 83 million dollars, while it continued to run them under a management contract. Hilton used part of the funds it received from the sale to reduce its long-term debt and repurchase some of the shares issued.

3. For example, Tharaldson Enterprises, Westmont Hospitality Group Inc., and Marcus Hotels & Resorts, which have 360, 287, and 199 hotels, respectively, run under management contracts. The said companies' entire portfolios are managed this way.

4. Conflicts can rapidly arise with this type of contract, as the owner wants quick returns on the money invested while the company running the hotel has a long-term vision, offering competitively low prices and high-quality service, so that the low initial profits increase as the volume of business grows during the long period of the contract's duration.

5. As the competition heats up between companies running hotels, more management companies enter the market, challenging the established ones by agreeing to accept lower fees, so that the amount of capital supplied by the hotel company will likely increase.

6. Although the company running the hotel cannot make such a profit as its owner when the business is doing well (because the profits are shared), it will lose less when it does poorly as the owner is the one who absorbs the hotel's losses.

7. This situation has been observed in some developing countries, such as Brazil, Hong Kong, India, and Singapore, where there has been an endogenous growth of the hotel sector, after several experiences in which multinationals have operated there under management contracts.

8. The GOP is defined as the gross earnings less all the normal running costs, except taxes levied on the property, insurance, rental costs, interest charges, repayments, and taxes on profits.

9. The Renaissance Hotels Group included the New World, Ramada (outside the United States), and Renaissance brand names.

10. For this reason, the company runs several training programs so that students can join Marriott and apply what they have learned to the workplace. These programs are offered for reception, catering, and accounting staff, among others. Marriott also offers the Marriott International MBA program.

11. Remember that until the takeovers of Westin and Sheraton, the company was considered a hotel owner, as most of its hotels were its own property.

12. This brand name's early growth in North America took the form of hotel ownership, even though initially the company expanded internationally by acquiring management contracts. Despite its franchise agreements being restricted to North America, company executives hoped that these agreements would act as the driving force behind its growth.

13. Westin had subsidiaries to manage its international operations, with one in Sao Paulo for its South American operations, another in Seattle for North America, another in Tokyo for Asia and the Pacific, and another in Hamburg for Europe.

14. In Spain, the following hotels came to form part of this group of properties: the Hotel Palace and the Santa María del Paular (both in Madrid), the Mencey (Santa Cruz de Tenerife), La Quinta (Marbella), Alfonso XIII (Seville), the María Cristina (San Sebastián), and the Arabella (Palma de Mallorca).

15. Its last big acquisition, the Spanish inner-city hotel chain Tryp Hoteles, was made up of hotels run solely under management contracts.

Chapter 11

1. The hotel chain is usually responsible for any repairs needed to conserve the buildings and facilities in good condition during the term of the contract, although it is normally not liable for the costs of any extraordinary repairs.

2. Remember that Best Western International is not a hotel chain but a hotel consortium.

Chapter 12

1. Between 1983 and 1985, for example, the following commercial names were introduced in the hotel industry alone: Renaissance, Esmerald Hotels, Ritz-Carlton, Royce Marriott's, Courtyards, Maquis, Holiday Inns, Embassy Suites, Brock Hotels, Residence Inns, Par Suites, Quality Inns, Trust House Forte's Exclusive, Excelsior, Viscounts, Wyndham Wynfield Inns, Compri, Sofitel, Novotel, Ibis, and Ciga.

2. By creating brands, company executives can position their products in certain markets. This is known as product positioning.

3. For example, a West German tourist might prefer the airline Lufthansa.

4. Brand consistency is easier to achieve at the cheaper end of the market than at the luxury end. Most of the design work and furnishings of hotels with less than two stars, such as Formule 1 and Motel 6 (both of which are owned by Accor), are standardized. In contrast, as a hotel increases its star rating, there is more variety in the type of building, room size, furniture, etc. At the super deluxe end of the market, there is no standard hotel product and the concept of personalized rooms takes over, i.e., rooms that are tailor-made for each client.

5. As an example of Super 8 Motels' quality, in February 1998 the hotel company Campbell Motel Properties Inc. decided to convert eleven of its thirty-five hotels into Super 8 franchise hotels, thus replacing its own "Travellers Inn" brand name.

6. These were originally three-star hotels, but, like Sofitel, they were forced to use a higher rating.

7. In the United States, Marriott and Hilton are the best-known brands in the top-range segment, with a level of brand recognition close to 50 percent and 40 percent, respectively, according to independent surveys. Marriott and Hilton have the greatest number of hotels in this segment, with more than 200 hotels each.

Chapter 13

1. A good way of achieving this is to learn from what other businesses do, incorporating this new knowledge, and improving on it. The learning potential that international operations offer is very important, because these operations are crucial in ensuring how competitive a business is.

2. The German experience (with very high wages and the deutschmark's normally strong exchange rate) and the Japanese experience both show that the quality of a product is a determining factor.

3. Some years ago, the Turkish government offered incentives to attract local and foreign investors to develop tourism businesses there (Baki, 1990).

4. For example, with the growth of charter airline companies, there was a rapid increase in traffic from North America to Europe, from Northern Europe to the Mediterranean, and, on a more limited scale, from Europe to more distant locations such as Kenya, Thailand, and the Caribbean. Later, jets with a higher passenger capacity increased both the speed and comfort of air travel and led to reductions in the prices of plane tickets (Heskett, 1986).

5. A tourism company's trademark guarantees a certain degree of quality, and this represents a big competitive edge over other companies, particularly when the latter offer clients a service in rather unappealing surroundings.

6. Companies can choose either to move along a learning curve that gradually changes from one approach to another, or not. Each approach suggests a particular corporate culture, organizational goals and strategies, and different structures.

7. A hotel company following this approach will tend to build its hotels in foreign markets that are highly similar to those of its country of origin.

8. The regional approach makes it possible to penetrate segments of the market that surpass national limits, thus increasing the possibility of economies of scale.

9. This method will give real estate businesses or European pension funds access to the tourist industry.

10. At present STI controls nine of Accor's Tunisian complexes, with a total of 5,000 beds: two are run under the Sofitel brand name and seven under the name Coralia Club. There are currently three new well-defined projects: the Sofitel Thalassa hotel in Djerba, the Novotel Aeropuerto in the capital, and the Sofitel Palais des Congress in Tunis, with a design similar to the company's hotel in Sydney. This last hotel has the backing of the Tunisian government.

11. Starwood Hotels & Resorts Worldwide converted thirteen of them into Four Points hotels, i.e., those in Newark and Piscataway (New Jersey); Pittsburgh (Pennsylvania); Oak Brook (Illinois); Burlington and Waltham (Massachusetts); Kansas

City (Missouri); Lexington (Kentucky); Denver (Colorado); Phoenix (Arizona); and three California locations: Culver City, Monrovia, and San Rafael. Another hotel in Annapolis (Maryland) will retain the Sheraton name. These hotels will keep the Barceló brand name in their titles (Barceló Four Points or Barceló Sheraton).

12. In 1990, Marriott International's portfolio in the region was limited to its Resort Marriott Casa Magna in Cancún, with 450 rooms, and to the Resort Marriott Casa Magna in Puerto Vallarta, with 433 rooms, both in Mexico.

Bibliography

Ader, J.N., La Fleur, R.A., Yurman, J.J., and McCoy, T. (2000). *Global lodging almanac.* New York: Bear Stearns.

Ajami, R.A. (1988). "Strategies for tourism transnationals in Belize." *Annals of Tourism Research,* 15(4), 517-530.

Ansoff, H.I. (1965). *Corporate strategy.* New York: McGraw-Hill.

Ansoff, H.I. (1976). *La estrategia de la empresa.* Navarre: Editorial Universidad de Navarra.

Arnold, D.E. (1987). "Study your market's actual needs." *Lodging,* 12(5), 37-38.

Auerbach, A.J. and Reishus, D. (1988). "Taxes and the merger decision." In Coffee, J., Lowenstein, L., and Ackerman, S.R. (eds.), *Knights, raiders and targets: The impact of the hostile takeover.* Oxford, UK: Oxford University Press.

Baki, A. (1990). "Turkey: Redeveloping tourism." *The Cornell Hotel and Restaurant Administration Quarterly,* 31(2), 60-64.

Biggadike, T. (1979). "The risk business of diversification." *Harvard Business Review,* May-June, 57(3), 103-111.

Calori, R. and Harvatopoulos, Y. (1988). "Diversification: Les règles de conduite." *Harvar-L'expansion,* Spring, 8-59.

Canals, J. (1992). *L'internacionalització.* Barcelona: Department of Industry.

Caves, R.E. (1989). "Mergers, takeovers and economic efficiency: Foresight vs. hindsight." *International Journal of Industrial Organization,* 7(1), 151-174.

Chandler, A. (1962). *Strategy and structure: Chapters in the history of the industrial enterprise.* Cambridge, MA: MIT Press.

Chandler, A. (1987). *The visible hand: The managerial revolution in American business.* Cambridge, MA: Harvard University Press.

Christenson, C.R., Andrews, K.R., and Bower, J.L. (1978). *Business policy: Text and cases.* Homewood, IL: Richard D. Irwin.

Crawford-Welch, S. (1991). "International marketing in the hospitality industry." In *Strategic hospitality management* (pp. 163-199). London: Cassell Publishing.

Cunill, O.M. (2002). Cadenas hotelas anelisis del top 10. Edited by Ariel Turismo. Madrid.

Daigne, J.F. (1986). *Dynamique du redressement d'entreprise.* Paris: Les Éditions d'Organisation.

Dawson, J. and Shaw, S. (1992). "Interfirm alliances in the retail sector: Evolutionary strategic and tactical issues in their creation and management." Working paper, series no. 9217. Department of Business Studies, Edinburgh University.

Dev, C. and Klein, S. (1993). "Strategic alliances in the hotel industry." *The Cornell Hotel and Restaurant Administration Quarterly,* (34), 42-45.

Dev, C. and Olsen, M. (1989). "Environmental uncertainty, business strategy and financial performance: An empirical study of the U.S. lodging industry." *Hospitality Education and Research Journal,* 13(3), 171-186.

Devling, G. and Bleackley, M. (1988). "Strategic alliances—Guidelines for success." *Long Range Planning,* 21(5), 18-23.

Drucker, P.F. (1975). *La nouvelle pratique de la direction des entreprises.* Paris: Les Éditions d'Organisation.

Dunning, J.H. (1981). *International production and the multinational enterprise.* London: Allen & Unwin.

Dunning, J.H. and McQueen, M. (1982). "Multinational corporations in the international hotel industry." *Annals of Tourism Research,* 9(1), 69-90.

Durán, J.J. (1977). *La diversificación como estrategia empresarial.* Madrid: Pirámide.

Fusiter, M. (1977). *Techniques de diversification de l'enterprise.* Paris: Hommes et Techniques.

Glueck, W.E. (1980). *Strategic management and business policy.* New York: McGraw-Hill.

Go, F., Pyo, S.S., Uysal, M., and Mihalik, B.J. (1990). "Decision criteria for transnational hotel expansion." *Tourism Management,* 11(4), 297-304.

Gort, M. (1969). "An economic disturbance theory of mergers." *Quarterly Journal of Economics,* 83, 624-642.

Harrigan, K.R. (1983). *Strategies for vertical integration.* Lanham, MD: Lexington Books.

Harrigan, K.R. (1985). *Strategies for joint ventures.* Lanham, MD: Lexington Books.

Harrigan, K.R. (1988). "Joint ventures and competitive strategy." *Strategic Management Journal,* 9, 141-158.

Heskett, J.L. (1986). *Managing in the service economy.* Boston: Harvard Business School Press.

Holderness, C.G. and Sheehan, D.P. (1985). "Raiders or saviours? The evidence on six controversial investors." *Journal of Financial Economics,* 14, 555-580.

International Franchise Association (IFA) (1991). "A study for the International Franchise Association." Washington, DC: Author.

Jacquemin, A. (1982). *Economía industrial.* Barcelona: Hispano Europea.

James, B.G. (1985). "Alliance: The new strategic focus." *Long Range Planning,* 18(3), 76-81.

James, R.M. (1987). "Pinpoint your product segment." *Lodging,* 12(5), 40-41.

Jarillo, J.C. (1990). *Dirección estratégica.* New York: McGraw-Hill.

Jarillo, J.C. and Martínez, J. (1991). *Estrategia internacional.* Madrid: McGraw-Hill.

Kaplan, Atid (1987). "The franchisor-franchisee relationship: Stronger partnership . . . greater growth." *Lodging,* 12(5), 47-48.

Kim, K. and Olsen, M. (1999). "Determinants of successful acquisition processes in the U.S. lodging industry." *International Journal of Hospitality Management,* 18(3), 285-308.

Kinch, J.E. and Hayes, J.P. (1986). *Franchising: The inside story.* Wilmington, DE: TriMark Publishing Co.

Kotler, P. (1988). *Marketing Management: Analysis, Planning, Implementation, and Control,* 6th Edition. Upper Saddle River, NJ: Pearson Education, Inc.

Kotler, P. (1996). *Dirección de marketing.* Upper Saddle River, NJ: Prentice Hall.

Levitt, T. (1983). "Relationship management." In *The marketing imagination.* New York: The Free Press.

Litteljohn, D. (1985). "Towards an economic analysis of trans/multinational hotel companies." *International Journal of Hospitality Management,* 4(4), 157-165.

Lowell, H.B. and Kirsch, M.A. (1991). "Growth by franchising: What both sides need to know." *Hotels,* 14(2), 50-52.

Mandigo, T.R. (1987). "Gauge the franchisor's support systems." *Lodging,* 12(5), 43-44.

Martín Rojo, I. (1988). "Crecimiento empresarial e internacionalización en el sector turístico." *Revista Información Hostelera,* December.

Martinet, A. C. (1983). *Stratégie.* Paris: Vuibert.

McGuffie, J. (1996). "Franchising in Europe." *EIU Travel and Tourism Analyst,* 1, 36-52.

McQueen, M. (1989). "Multinationals in tourism." In Witt, Stephen F. and Moutinho, Luiz (eds.), *Tourism marketing and management handbook* (pp. 285-289). New York: Prentice Hall.

Mintzberg, H. and Quinn, J.B. (1993). *El priceso estrategico: Conceptos, contextos y casos.* Mexico: Prentice Hall.

Morvan, Y. (1985). *Fondements d'economie industrielle.* Paris: Economica.

Mueller, D.C. (1989). "Mergers: Causes, effects and policies." *International Journal of Industrial Organization,* 7(1), 1-10.

Myro, R. (1999). "Tendencias recientes de la inversión internacional." XIV Jornadas de Economía Española, Alicante University, October 1999, Alicante.

Naisbitt Group, The (1989). The future of franchising. Washington, DC: Uniform Franchise Offering Circular.

Newman, W.H., Logan, J.P., and Hegarty, W.H. (1989). *Strategy: A multi-level, integrative approach.* Cincinnati, OH: South-Western Publishing.

Ohmae, K. (1991). *Triad power: The coming shape of global competition.* New York: The Free Press.

Olsen, M., Damonte, T., and Jackson, G.A. (1989). "Segmentation in the lodging industry: Is it doomed to failure?" *American Hotel and Motel Association Newsletter.*

Pérez Moriones, A. (1998). *El contrato de gestión hotelera.* Valencia: Tirant lo blanch.

Perlmutter, H.J. (1967). "Social architectural problems of the multinational firm." *Quarterly Journal of AIESEC International,* 3(3).

Porter, M. (1982). *Competitive strategy: Techniques for analyzing industries and competitors.* New York: The Free Press.

Porter, M. (1986). "Changing patterns of international competition." *California Management Review,* 28(2), 9-40.

Ramanujan, V. and Varadajan, P. (1989). "Research on corporate diversification: A synthesis." *Strategic Management Journal,* 10, 523-555.

Ravenscraft, D.J. and Scherer, F.M. (1989). "The profitability of mergers," *International Journal of Industrial Organization,* 7(1).

Robinson, E.A.G. (1957). *The structure of competitive industry.* Chicago, IL: University of Chicago Press.

Rochet, C. (1981). *Diversification et redeploiment de l'entrepise.* Paris: Les Éditions d'Organisation.

Rumelt, R.P. (1974). *Strategy, structure and economic performance.* Cambridge, MA: Harvard Business School.

Sharma, D.D. (1984). "Management contracts and international marketing industrial goods." In *International marketing management.* New York: Praeger.

Slattery, P., in Kleinwort Benson Research (1988). *International Hospitality Review.* Tunbridge Wells, UK: Patterson Printing.

Strategor (1988). *Stratégie, structure, décision, identité.* Paris: Intereditions. (Spanish edition: *Estrategia, estructura, decisión, identidad,* [1995], Biblio empresa.)

Tilles, S. (1963). "How to evaluate corporate strategy." *Harvard Business Review,* July-August, 41(4), 111-121.

Trautwein, F. (1990). "Merger motives and merger prescriptions." *Strategic Management Journal,* (11)4, 283-295.

UNCTC (1988). "Transnational corporations in world development: Trends and prospects." New York: United Nations Center for Transnational Corporations World Bank, June 1972. Tourism Sector Working Paper, Washington, DC; World Bank Group.

Vernon-Wortzel, J. and Wortzel, L.H. (1991). *Global strategic management.* New York: John Wiley.

West, J.J. and Olsen M. (1989). "Competitive tactics in food service: Are high performers different?" *The Cornell Hotel and Restaurant Administration Quarterly,* 30, 68-71.

Whitford, M. (1998). "Merger and acquisition activity dominates lodging landscape." *Hotel and Motel Management,* September, 213, 48-67.

Williamson, O.E. (1975). *Markets and hierarchies: Analysis and antitrust implications.* London: The Free Press.

Williamson, O.E. (1986). *Economic organizations: Firms, markets and policy control.* Brighton, UK: Wheatsheaf Books.

Withiam, G. (1985). "Hotel companies aim for multiple markets." *The Cornell Hotel and Restaurant Administration Quarterly,* (November), 39-51.

Witt, S.F., Brooke, M.Z., and Buckley, P.J. (1991). *The management of international tourism.* London: Unwin Hyman.

Wright, P. (1987). "A refinement of Porter's strategies." *Strategic Management Journal,* 8, 93-101.

Yesawich, P., in Withiam G. (1985). "Hotel companies aim for multiple markets." *The Cornell Hotel and Restaurant Administration Quarterly,* 26, 39-51.

Ziff-Levine, W. (1990). "The cultural logic gap: A Japanese tourism research experience." *Tourism Management,* 11(2), 105-110.

Index

Page numbers followed by the letter "f" indicate a figure; those followed by the letter "t" indicate a table.

Absorption, definition, 75
Accor
    alliance with Amorim, 107
    cost leadership strategy, 11
    diversification strategy, 30
    franchising, 124, 125t
    horizontal integration, 59t, 60t, 61
    internationalization-globalization,
        181-182
    management contracts, 135, 136t
    vertical integration, 45-46
Acquisition, definition, 75
Acquisitions, 73-80
    in accommodation industry, 82t-91t
    advantages, 79-80
    examples, 80-81, 91-93
    implications, 79-80
    theories, 75-78, 76f
Affair, strategic alliance as, 100
Airtours, vertical integration, 44-45
Alliance, marketing, 28
America Online (AOL), 47
American Express, 71
Amorim, alliance with Accor, 107
Ansoff, H.I., 17, 55
    growth vector matrix, 18
AOL Avant, 47
Argentaria, 71
    joint venture with Grupo Barceló
        and FCC, 107
Avis, 27

B2B Internet portal, 107-108
Backward vertical integration, 39, 41
Barceló Empresas
    B2B Internet portal, 107-108
    diagonal integration, 71
    vertical integration, 46
Basic fee or incentive fee system, 132
Basic fee plus incentive fee system, 132
Basic fee system, 132
Best Western International
    branding, 157-158
    horizontal integration, 59t, 60t, 62-63
    internationalization-globalization,
        184
Biggadike, T., 24
Bollenbach, Steven, 33
Brand, 149
Brand name, 150
Brand ownership, five types, 152-153
Brand symbol, 150
Branding, 149-157
    advantages, 153-154
    Best Western International, 157-158
    biggest hotel brands, 158t, 165t-166t
    Comfort Inn, 160
    Courtyard by Marriott, 163
    Days Inn, 159
    differentiation, 157
    disadvantages, 154-155
    Express by Holiday Inn, 161
    Hampton Inn & Suites, 160-161

Branding *(continued)*
  Hilton Hotels, 162
  Holiday Inn, 158-159
  Hyatt Regency, 164
  Ibis, 164
  internationalization, 157
  Marriott Hotels, Resorts & Suites, 159
  Mercure, 163
  Motel 6, 162
  Novotel, 164
  Quality, 163
  Radisson Hotels & Resorts, 161
  Ramada Franchise Systems, 160
  Sheraton Hotels & Resorts, 160
  Super 8 Motels, 160
  Top 10 hotel chains, 166-167
Brand-related decisions, 151t
Bulgari SpA, joint venture with Marriott International, 106
Business travel, market niche strategy, 15
Business-format franchising, 111-112

C&N, 108
Caixa Galicia, 108
Canals, Jordi, 172
Capital Logistics, 27
Carlson Hospitality Worldwide
  differentiation strategy, 14
  diversification strategy, 32
  horizontal integration, 59t, 60t, 63-64
  internationalization-globalization, 186-187
  vertical integration, 45
Cendant Corporation
  cost leadership strategy, 10-11
  diversification strategy, 26-29
  franchising, 118-120
  horizontal integration, 58, 59t, 60t
  joint venture with Marriott International, 106
  vertical integration, 46-47

Chain versus independent hotels, 56-57.
  See also Horizontal integration
Chandler, A., 17
Choice Hotels International
  cost leadership strategy, 12
  franchising, 120-122, 122t
  horizontal integration, 59t, 60t, 61-62
  internationalization-globalization, 188
  and strategic alliance, 105-106
Co-branding, 152
Comfort Inn, branding, 160
Competitive strategy, 5-10
  applying, 9-10
  forces affecting, 6f
  generic, three, 7f
Complementary leisure services, InterContinental, 29
Concentric diversification, 22
Conglomerate diversification, 22
Conversion franchising, 112
Cook, Thomas, 43
Coordinating advantages, 175
Copyright, 150
Cost leadership strategy, 7
  Accor, 11
  Cendant Corporation, 10-11
  Choice Hotels International, 12
  Hilton Hotel Corporation, 12
  InterContinental, 12
  Marriott International, 12
Courtyard by Marriott, branding, 163
Cross-franchising operation, 101
Cruise lines, 35
Cultural core, 25

Daughter company, 101, 102
Days Inn, 11
  branding, 159
Diagonal integration, 69-70
  examples of, 71-72
Díaz, Gerardo, 48
Differentiation, branding strategy, 157

Differentiation strategy, 8-9
    Carlson Hospitality Worldwide, 14
    Four Seasons, 13
    Hilton Hotels Corporations, 14
    Hyatt, 13
    InterContinental, 14
    Marriott International, 13
    Shangri-La, 14
    Sol Meliá, 14
    Starwood Hotels & Resorts
        Worldwide, 13
Diversification strategy, 17-26
    Accor, 30
    Carlson Hospitality Worldwide, 32
    Cendant Corporation, 26-29
    InterContinental, 29
    Marriott International, 30-32
Dorint Hotels, alliance with Six
        Continents, 107
Drucker, P.F., 26
Dunning, J.H., 173

Econo Lodge, 12
Economic disturbance theory, 78
Economies of scope, 69, 70
Efficiency theory, 75
Empire-building theory, 77
Endorsement, brand ownership, 152
Entrepreneur, 53
Entry barrier, 7
Escarrer, Sebastián, 48
Etap, 11
Ethnocentrism, 176
Express by Holiday Inn, branding, 161
Extended Stay America, management
        contracts, 135-136
External growth, 73-74

Fairfield Inn, 12
FCC (Fomento de Construcciones y
        Contratas), 71
    joint venture with Grupo Barceló
        and Argentaria, 107

Fees, franchising, 116-117
    Choice Hotels International, 122t
    Hilton Hotels Corporation, 125t
    Six Continents PLC, 123t
Fees, management contracts, 131-132
Finance, chain versus independent
        hotels, 57
Financial synergies, 75
First Choice, vertical integration, 46
Fluctuation, market, 55
Focus strategy, 9
Forecasts, 55
Formule 1, 11
Forte, Sir Rocco, 65-66
Forward vertical integration, 39, 41
Four Seasons, differentiation strategy, 13
Franchisee, 111, 115-116
Franchiser, 111, 114-115
Franchising, 111-117
    Accor, 124, 125t
    Cendant Corporation, 118-120
    Choice Hotels International,
        120-122, 122t
    Hilton Hotels Corporation, 123-124,
        124t, 125t
    Six Continents PLC, 123, 123t
    Top 10, 117t

Gateway cities, 176-177
Geocentrism, 176
Geographical expansion, 19
Global Distribution System (GDS), 47
Global orientation, 176
Globalization, hotel chains, 169-178,
        170f, 171f
    Accor, 181-182
    Best Western International, 184
    Carlson Hospitality Worldwide,
        186-187
    Choice Hotels International, 188
    Golden Tulip Hotels, Inns &
        Resorts, 187-188
    Hilton Group PLC, 184-185
    InterContinental, 180-181

Globalization, hotel chains *(continued)*
  Le Méridien Hotels & Resorts, 187
  Marriott International, 185-186
  Starwood Hotels & Resorts
      Worldwide, 183-184
  Top 10, 179f
Golden Tulip Hotels, Inns & Resorts,
    internationalization-
    globalization, 187-188
Growth vector matrix, Ansoff, 18
Grubarges Inversión, 71
Grupo Barceló, joint venture with FCC
    and Argentaria, 107
Grupo Globalia, vertical integration, 49
Grupo Iberostar, vertical integration,
    48-49
Grupo Marsans, vertical integration, 48
Grupotel, alliance with TUI, 108

Hampton Inn & Suites, branding,
    160-161
Harrigan, K.R., 38, 42, 102
Henderson, Ernest, 56-57
Heterogeneous diversification, 22
Hilton group, PLC,
    internationalization-
    globalization, 184-185
Hilton Hotels Corporation
  alliance with Hilton International,
      104-105
  branding, 162
  cost leadership strategy, 12
  differentiation strategy, 14
  franchising, 123-124, 124t, 125t
  horizontal integration, 59t, 60t, 62
  management contracts, 139-140,
      141t
  specialization strategy, 33
Hilton International, alliance with
    Hilton Hotels Corporation,
    104-105
Holiday Inn
  branding, 158-159
  franchising, 113

Home-country orientation, 176
Homogenous diversification, 22
Horizontal diversification, 22
Horizontal integration, 51
  Accor, 59t, 60t, 61
  analysis of hotel industry's, 64-68
  Best Western International, 59t, 60t,
      62-63
  Carlson Hospitality Worldwide, 59t,
      60t, 63-64
  Cendant Corporation, 58, 59t, 60t
  Choice Hotels International, 59t,
      60t, 61-62
  financial factors, 54
  Hilton Hotels Corporation, 59t, 60t, 62
  management factors, 53
  Marriott International, 59t, 60-61, 60t
  risk factors, 55-58
  sales factor, 54-55
  Six Continents Hotels, 59, 59t, 60t
  Sol Meliá, 59t, 60t, 64
  Starwood Hotels & Resorts
      Worldwide, 59t, 60t, 63
  technical factors, 52-53
Horizontal joint venture, 102
Host-country orientation, 176
Hub-and-spoke strategy, 177
Hyatt, differentiation strategy, 13
Hyatt Regency, branding, 164

I do, strategic alliance, 100
Ibercaja, 108
Iberia
  joint venture with Sol Meliá, 107
  vertical integration, 47-48
Iberostar, 107-108
Ibis, branding, 164
Initial fee, franchising, 116
InterContinental
  cost leadership strategy, 12
  differentiation strategy, 14
  diversification strategy, 29
  internationalization-globalization,
      180-181

Internal growth, 73-74
International diversification, 19
Internationalization, branding strategy, 157
Internationalization, hotel chains, 169-178, 170f, 171f
  Accor, 181-182
  Best Western International, 184
  Carlson Hospitality Worldwide, 186-187
  Choice Hotels International, 188
  Golden Tulip Hotels, Inns & Resorts, 187-188
  Hilton Group PLC, 184-185
  InterContinental, 180-181
  Le Méridien Hotels & Resorts, 187
  Marriott International, 185-186
  Starwood Hotels & Resorts Worldwide, 183-184
  Top 10, 179f
Inversora de Hoteles Vacacionales SA, 108

Japan Airlines (JAL), 49
Joint venture, 78-79, 101-103, 102f
  examples, 104-108
  failure of, 98
  horizontal, 102
  vertical, 102

Knights Inn, 11

La Méridien Hotels & Resorts, internationalization-globalization, 187
Large-scale purchases, 55
Leaseholds, 145-146, 147t
  examples, 147-148
Limited service segment, market niche strategy, 15
Live essentials, Accor, 30

Location-specific advantages, 174-175
Long-stay segment, market niche strategy, 15

Management contracts, 127-132
  Accor, 135, 136t
  Extended Stay America, 135-136
  fees, 131-132
  Hilton Hotels Corporation, 139-140, 141t
  management company, advantages/disadvantages, 130-131
  Marriott International, 134-135
  owner, advantages/disadvantages, 131
  Prime Hospitality, 140-141
  Six continents Hotels, 137-138
  Société du Louvre, 137
  Sol Meliá, 141-142, 143t
  Starwood Hotels & Resorts Worldwide, 138-139
  Tharaldson enterprises, 136-137
  Top 10, 133t
  Westmont Hospitality Group, 138
Management synergies, 75
Management-rotation system, 25
Market internalization, 175
Market niche strategy, 9, 15
Marketing diversification, 19
Marketing fee, franchising, 116
Marriott Hotels, Resorts & Suites, branding, 159
Marriott International
  cost leadership strategy, 12
  differentiation strategy, 13
  diversification strategy, 30-32
  horizontal integration, 59t, 60-61, 60t
  internationalization-globalization, 185-186
  joint venture with Bulgari SpA, 106
  joint venture with Cendant Corporation, 106
  management contracts, 134-135

Mercure, branding, 163
Mergers, 73-80
    in accommodation industry, 82t-91t
    advantages, 79-80
    examples, 80-81, 91-93
    implications, 79-80
    theories, 75-78, 76f
"Merton's conjecture," 80
"Mid position," 10
Mintzberg, H., 1-2
Mitchell and Butlers division,
        InterContinental, 29
Monolithic, brand ownership, 152
Monopoly theory, 76-77
Motel 6, 11
    branding, 162
Multibranding, 155
Multiple, brand ownership, 152-153
Myro, R., 80

Nikko, vertical integration, 49
Novotel, branding, 164

One-night stand, strategic alliance, 100
Operational synergies, 75
Ownership, hotel, 146, 147t
    examples, 147-148
Ownership advantage, 173-174

"Paired share" status, 80
Pascual, Gonzalo, 48
Performance, Accor improving, 30
PHH Arval, 27
Polycentrism, 176
Porter, M., 5
Preussag, vertical integration, 43-44
Prime Hospitality, management
        contracts, 140-141
Process balancing, 52-53
Process theory, 77-78
Product franchising, 111

Profit Impact of Market Strategy
        (PIMS), 38
Profit Manager, Choice Hotels
        International, 121
Promotion, chain versus independent
        hotels, 57
Purchases, chain versus independent
        hotels, 57
Pure diversification, 22
Pure franchiser, 117
Pure hotel chain, Hilton, 33

Quality, branding, 163
Quinn, James Brian, 1

Radisson Hotels & Resorts, branding, 161
Raider theory, 77
Ramada Franchise Systems, branding, 160
Real estate division, Cendant
        Corporation, 27-28
Real estate investment trusts (REITs), 80
Red Roof Inn, 11
Regiocentrism, 176
Regional orientation, 176
Registered trademark, 150
Relocation services, Cendant, 28
Reservation fee, franchising, 116
Resort Condominium International
        (RCI), 27
Roadside service segment, market
        niche strategy, 15
Robinson, E.A.G., 51, 53
Rodeway Inn, 12
Rumelt, R.P., 38

Sa Nostra, 108
Schorghuber Corporate, joint venture
        with Starwood Hotels &
        Resorts Worldwide, 106
Senior living centers, 35
Shangri-La, differentiation strategy, 14
Sheraton Hotels & Resorts, branding, 160

Six Continents Hotels
  alliance with Dorint Hotels, 107
  franchising, 123, 123t
  horizontal integration, 59, 59t, 60t
  management contracts, 137-138
Sleep Inn, 12
Société du Louvre, management
    contracts, 137
Sol Meliá
  B2B Internet portal, 107-108
  differentiation strategy, 14
  horizontal integration, 59t, 60t, 64
  joint venture with Iberia, 107
  management contracts, 141-142, 143t
  vertical integration, 47-48
Specialization strategy, 18, 33-35. *See
    also* Diversification strategy
SpringHill Suites, 12
Staff, chain versus independent hotels, 57
Starwood Hotels & Resorts Worldwide
  differentiation strategy, 13
  horizontal integration, 59t, 60t, 63-64
  internationalization-globalization,
      183-184
  joint venture with Schorghuber
      Corporate, 106
  management contracts, 138-139
  specialization strategy, 33
Strategic alliance, 95-104
  advantages, 100-101
  examples, 104-108
  process, 99f
  strategies, 98f
Strategy, 1-3
Strong brands, 156
Super 8 Motels, 10
  branding, 160
Synergies, 21, 24, 55-56, 69, 70
  acquisitions/mergers, 75
Systems gains, 69, 70

Telefónica, 107-108
Tharaldson Enterprises, management
    contracts, 136-137

Time share, 34-35
  Marriott International, 31
"Total Lodging by Choice," 121
TownePlace Suites, 12
Trautwein, F., 77-78
Travelodge Hotel, 11
TUI, alliance with Grupotel, 108

Umbrella, brand ownership, 152
Uncertain demand, 102, 103f
United Airlines, 71

Valuation theory, 77
Value chain, 6
Variable fee, franchising, 116
Venture capital company, 97
Vertical disintegration, 41
Vertical diversification, 22
Vertical integration, 37-43
  Accor, 45-46
  Airtours, 44-45
  Barceló Empresas, 46
  Carlson Hospitality Worldwide, 45
  Cendant Corporation, 46-47
  First Choice, 46
  Grupo Globalia, 49
  Grupo Iberostar, 48-49
  Grupo Marsans, 48
  Iberia, 47-48
  Nikko, 49
  Preussag, 43-44
  Sol Meliá, 47-48
Vertical joint venture, 102
Viva Tours, 47

Well-being, Accor enhancing, 30
Westmont Hospitality Group,
        management contracts, 138
Williamson, O.E., 95
Wright, P., 10

Yearly fee, franchising, 116

THE HAWORTH HOSPITALITY PRESS®
Hospitality, Travel, and Tourism
K. S. Chon, PhD, Editor in Chief

CULTURAL TOURISM: GLOBAL AND LOCAL PERSPECTIVES edited by Greg Richards. (2007).

GAY TOURISM: CULTURE AND CONTEXT by Gordon Waitt and Kevin Markwell. (2006).

CASES IN SUSTAINABLE TOURISM: AN EXPERIENTIAL APPROACH TO MAKING DECISIONS edited by Irene M. Herremans. (2006). "As a tourism instructor and researcher, I recommend this textbook for both undergraduate and graduate students who wish to pursue their careers in parks, recreation, or tourism. The text is appropriate both for junior and senior tourism management classes and graduate classes. It is an excellent primer for understanding the fundamental concepts, issues, and real-world examples of sustainable tourism." *HwanSuk Chrus Choi, PhD, Assistant Professor, School of Hospitality and Tourism Management, University of Gueph*

COMMUNITY DESTINATION MANAGEMENT IN DEVELOPING ECONOMIES edited by Walter Jamieson. (2006). "This book is a welcome and valuable addition to the destination management literature, focusing as it does on developing economies in the Asian context. It provides an unusually comprehensive and informative overview of critical issues in the field, effectively combining well-crafted discussions of key conceptual and methodological issues with carefully selected and well-presented case studies drawn from a number of contrasting Asian destinations." *Peter Hills, PhD, Professor and Director, The Centre of Urban Planning and Environmental Management, The University of Hong Kong*

MANAGING SUSTAINABLE TOURISM: A LEGACY FOR THE FUTURE by David L. Edgell Sr. (2006). "This comprehensive book on sustainable tourism should be required reading for everyone interested in tourism. The author is masterful in defining strategies and using case studies to explain best practices in generating long-term economic return on your tourism investment." *Kurtis M. Ruf, Partner, Ruf Strategic Solutions; Author,* Contemporary Database Marketing

CASINO INDUSTRY IN ASIA PACIFIC: DEVELOPMENT, OPERATION, AND IMPACT edited by Cathy H.C. Hsu. (2006). "This book is a must-read for anyone interested in the opportunities and challenges that the proliferation of casino gaming will bring to Asia in the early twenty-first century. The economic and social consequences of casino gaming in Asia may ultimately prove to be far more significant than those encountered in the West, and this book opens the door as to what those consequences might be." *William R. Eadington, PhD, Professor of Economics and Director, Institute for the Study of Gambling and Commercial Gaming, University of Nevada, Reno*

THE GROWTH STRATEGIES OF HOTEL CHAINS: BEST BUSINESS PRACTICES BY LEADING COMPANIES by Onofre Martorell Cunill. (2006). "Informative, well-written, and up-to-date. This is one title that I shall certainly be adding to my 'must-read' list for students this year." *Tom Baum, PhD, Professor of International Tour-*

ism and Hospitality Management, The Scottish Hotel School, The University of Strath-clyde, Glasgow

HANDBOOK FOR DISTANCE LEARNING IN TOURISM by Gary Williams. (2005). "This is an important book for a variety of audiences. As a resource for educational designers (and their managers) in particular, it is invaluable. The book is easy to read, and is full of practical information that can be logically applied in the design and development of flexible learning resources." *Louise Berg, MA, DipED, Lecturer in Education, Charles Sturt University, Australia*

VIETNAM TOURISM by Arthur Asa Berger. (2005). "Fresh and innovative…. Drawing upon Professor Berger's background and experience in cultural studies, this book offers an imaginative and personal portrayal of Vietnam as a tourism destination…. A very welcome addition to the field of destination studies." *Professor Brian King, PhD, Head, School of Hospitality, Tourism & Marketing, Victoria University, Australia*

TOURISM AND HOTEL DEVELOPMENT IN CHINA: FROM POLITICAL TO ECONOMIC SUCCESS by Hanqin Qiu Zhang, Ray Pine, and Terry Lam. (2005). "This is one of the most comprehensive books on China tourism and hotel development. It is one of the best textbooks for educators, students, practitioners, and investors who are interested in china tourism and hotel industry. Readers will experience vast, diversified, and past and current issues that affect every educator, student, practitioner, and investor in China tourism and hotel globally in an instant." *Hailin Qu, PhD, Full Professor and William E. Davis Distinguished Chair, School of Hotel & Restaurant Administration, Oklahoma State University*

THE TOURISM AND LEISURE INDUSTRY: SHAPING THE FUTURE edited by Klaus Weiermair and Christine Mathies. (2004). "If you need or want to know about the impact of globalization, the impact of technology, societal forces of change, the experience economy, adaptive technologies, environmental changes, or the new trend of slow tourism, you need this book. *The Tourism and Leisure Industry* contains a great mix of research and practical information." *Charles R. Goeldner, PhD, Professor Emeritus of Marketing and Tourism, Leeds School of Business, University of Colorado*

OCEAN TRAVEL AND CRUISING: A CULTURAL ANALYSIS by Arthur Asa Berger. (2004). "Dr. Berger presents an interdisciplinary discussion of the cruise industry for the thinking person. This is an enjoyable social psychology travel guide with a little business management thrown in. A great book for the curious to read a week before embarking on a first cruise or for the frequent cruiser to gain a broader insight into exactly what a cruise experience represents." *Carl Braunlich, DBA, Associate Professor, Department of Hospitality and Tourism Management, Purdue University, West Lafayette, Indiana*

STANDING THE HEAT: ENSURING CURRICULUM QUALITY IN CULINARY ARTS AND GASTRONOMY by Joseph A. Hegarty. (2003). "This text provides the genesis of a well-researched, thoughtful, rigorous, and sound theoretical framework for the enlargement and expansion of higher education programs in culinary arts and gastronomy." *John M. Antun, PhD, Founding Director, National Restaurant Institute, School of Hotel, Restaurant, and Tourism Management, University of South Carolina*

SEX AND TOURISM: JOURNEYS OF ROMANCE, LOVE, AND LUST edited by Thomas G. Bauer and Bob McKercher. (2003). "Anyone interested in or concerned about the impact of tourism on society and particularly in the developing world, should read this book. It explores a subject that has long remained ignored, almost a taboo area for many governments, institutions, and organizations. It demonstrates that the stereotyping of 'sex tourism' is too simple and travel and sex have many manifestations. The book follows its theme in an innovative and original way." *Carson L. Jenkins, PhD, Professor of International Tourism, University of Strathclyde, Glasgow, Scotland*

CONVENTION TOURISM: INTERNATIONAL RESEARCH AND INDUSTRY PERSPECTIVES edited by Karin Weber and Kye-Sung Chon. (2002). "This comprehensive book is truly global in its perspective. The text points out areas of needed research—a great starting point for graduate students, university faculty, and industry professionals alike. While the focus is mainly academic, there is a lot of meat for this burgeoning industry to chew on as well." *Patti J. Shock, CPCE, Professor and Department Chair, Tourism and Convention Administration, Harrah College of Hotel Administration, University of Nevada–Las Vegas*

CULTURAL TOURISM: THE PARTNERSHIP BETWEEN TOURISM AND CULTURAL HERITAGE MANAGEMENT by Bob McKercher and Hilary du Cros. (2002). "The book brings together concepts, perspectives, and practicalities that must be understood by both cultural heritage and tourism managers, and as such is a must-read for both." *Hisashi B. Sugaya, AICP, Former Chair, International Council of Monuments and Sites, International Scientific Committee on Cultural Tourism; Former Executive Director, Pacific Asia Travel Association Foundation, San Francisco, CA*

TOURISM IN THE ANTARCTIC: OPPORTUNITIES, CONSTRAINTS, AND FUTURE PROSPECTS by Thomas G. Bauer. (2001). "Thomas Bauer presents a wealth of detailed information on the challenges and opportunities facing tourism operators in this last great tourism frontier." *David Mercer, PhD, Associate Professor, School of Geography & Environmental Science, Monash University, Melbourne, Australia*

SERVICE QUALITY MANAGEMENT IN HOSPITALITY, TOURISM, AND LEISURE edited by Jay Kandampully, Connie Mok, and Beverley Sparks. (2001). "A must-read. . . . a treasure. . . . pulls together the work of scholars across the globe, giving you access to new ideas, international research, and industry examples from around the world." *John Bowen, Professor and Director of Graduate Studies, William F. Harrah College of Hotel Administration, University of Nevada, Las Vegas*

TOURISM IN SOUTHEAST ASIA: A NEW DIRECTION edited by K. S. (Kaye) Chon. (2000). "Presents a wide array of very topical discussions on the specific challenges facing the tourism industry in Southeast Asia. A great resource for both scholars and practitioners." *Dr. Hubert B. Van Hoof, Assistant Dean/Associate Professor, School of Hotel and Restaurant Management, Northern Arizona University*

THE PRACTICE OF GRADUATE RESEARCH IN HOSPITALITY AND TOURISM edited by K. S. Chon. (1999). "An excellent reference source for students pursuing graduate degrees in hospitality and tourism." *Connie Mok, PhD, CHE, Associate Professor, Conrad N. Hilton College of Hotel and Restaurant Management, University of Houston, Texas*

THE INTERNATIONAL HOSPITALITY MANAGEMENT BUSINESS: MANAGEMENT AND OPERATIONS by Larry Yu. (1999). "The abundant real-world examples and cases provided in the text enable readers to understand the most up-to-date developments in international hospitality business." *Zheng Gu, PhD, Associate Professor, College of Hotel Administration, University of Nevada, Las Vegas*

CONSUMER BEHAVIOR IN TRAVEL AND TOURISM by Abraham Pizam and Yoel Mansfeld. (1999). "A must for anyone who wants to take advantage of new global opportunities in this growing industry." *Bonnie J. Knutson, PhD, School of Hospitality Business, Michigan State University*

LEGALIZED CASINO GAMING IN THE UNITED STATES: THE ECONOMIC AND SOCIAL IMPACT edited by Cathy H. C. Hsu. (1999). "Brings a fresh new look at one of the areas in tourism that has not yet received careful and serious consideration in the past." *Muzaffer Uysal, PhD, Professor of Tourism Research, Virginia Polytechnic Institute and State University, Blacksburg*

HOSPITALITY MANAGEMENT EDUCATION edited by Clayton W. Barrows and Robert H. Bosselman. (1999). "Takes the mystery out of how hospitality management education programs function and serves as an excellent resource for individuals interested in pursuing the field." *Joe Perdue, CCM, CHE, Director, Executive Masters Program, College of Hotel Administration, University of Nevada, Las Vegas*

MARKETING YOUR CITY, U.S.A.: A GUIDE TO DEVELOPING A STRATEGIC TOURISM MARKETING PLAN by Ronald A. Nykiel and Elizabeth Jascolt. (1998). "An excellent guide for anyone involved in the planning and marketing of cities and regions. . . . A terrific job of synthesizing an otherwise complex procedure." *James C. Maken, PhD, Associate Professor, Babcock Graduate School of Management, Wake Forest University, Winston-Salem, North Carolina*

Order a copy of this book with this form or online at:
http://www.haworthpress.com/store/product.asp?sku=5387

THE GROWTH STRATEGIES OF HOTEL CHAINS
Best Business Practices by Leading Companies

_____in hardbound at $49.95 (ISBN-13: 978-0-7890-2663-7; ISBN-10: 0-7890-2663-5)

_____in softbound at $24.95 (ISBN-13: 978-0-7890-2664-4; ISBN-10: 0-7890-2664-3)

Or order online and use special offer code HEC25 in the shopping cart.

COST OF BOOKS_____	☐ **BILL ME LATER:** (Bill-me option is good on US/Canada/Mexico orders only; not good to jobbers, wholesalers, or subscription agencies.)
	☐ Check here if billing address is different from
POSTAGE & HANDLING_____	shipping address and attach purchase order and
(US: $4.00 for first book & $1.50	billing address information.
for each additional book)	
(Outside US: $5.00 for first book	Signature_____
& $2.00 for each additional book)	
SUBTOTAL_____	☐ **PAYMENT ENCLOSED: $**_____
IN CANADA: ADD 7% GST_____	☐ **PLEASE CHARGE TO MY CREDIT CARD.**
STATE TAX_____	☐ Visa ☐ MasterCard ☐ AmEx ☐ Discover
(NJ, NY, OH, MN, CA, IL, IN, PA, & SD	☐ Diner's Club ☐ Eurocard ☐ JCB
residents, add appropriate local sales tax)	Account #_____
FINAL TOTAL_____	Exp. Date_____
(If paying in Canadian funds,	
convert using the current	Signature_____
exchange rate, UNESCO	
coupons welcome)	

Prices in US dollars and subject to change without notice.

NAME_____

INSTITUTION_____

ADDRESS_____

CITY_____

STATE/ZIP_____

COUNTRY_____ COUNTY (NY residents only)_____

TEL_____ FAX_____

E-MAIL_____

May we use your e-mail address for confirmations and other types of information? ☐ Yes ☐ No
We appreciate receiving your e-mail address and fax number. Haworth would like to e-mail or fax special discount offers to you, as a preferred customer. **We will never share, rent, or exchange your e-mail address or fax number.** We regard such actions as an invasion of your privacy.

Order From Your Local Bookstore or Directly From
The Haworth Press, Inc.
10 Alice Street, Binghamton, New York 13904-1580 • USA
TELEPHONE: 1-800-HAWORTH (1-800-429-6784) / Outside US/Canada: (607) 722-5857
FAX: 1-800-895-0582 / Outside US/Canada: (607) 771-0012
E-mail to: orders@haworthpress.com

For orders outside US and Canada, you may wish to order through your local
sales representative, distributor, or bookseller.
For information, see http://haworthpress.com/distributors

(Discounts are available for individual orders in US and Canada only, not booksellers/distributors.)
PLEASE PHOTOCOPY THIS FORM FOR YOUR PERSONAL USE.
http://www.HaworthPress.com   BOF04